In
Tusca
Umbria

Jarrold Publishing

CONTENTS

Title page: Siena

San Gimignano

Introducing Tuscany and Umbria

Tuscany and Umbria: an idyllic blend of art and nature. If that is what you ask of a holiday, you will find everything you want here in the heart of Italy.

Tuscany is almost synonymous with the spirit of humanism, Umbria with the spirit of contemplation. A visitor who understands these age-old points of reference is assured of a splendid holiday, not exhausting or overwhelming, but 'vital' in the truest sense of the word, a refreshment of both body and soul at the end of a hard year's work.

Every thirty kilometres or so comes one of those ancient towns, some large, some small, whose names are familiar from schooldays, embodiments of the northerner's perennial yearning for the south: Florence and Siena, Pisa, Lucca, Arezzo, Orvieto, Perugia... There are places like Elba, and the Isola del Giglio (the 'island of lilies'), the woods of Umbria, the ridges of the Apennines, places of pilgrimage in the steps of St Francis of Assisi, and Norcia, the birthplace of Benedict of Nursia.

First to strike the eye are the colours which make up the mosaic of these two landscapes: the silvery-olive of Tuscany and the green of Umbria, the red soil of Siena chequered in summer with fields of yellow wheat, the blue of the Maremma beaches, the snowy whiteness of the Carrara marble-quarries and the weathered grey of the castles — a variety of hues which sharpen the senses for the feast of art and architecture to be found in the towns and cities. It is impossible to take in everything. Tuscany

Chianti country

and Umbria are one continuous 'sight', a great open-air museum.

Turn off along one of the small country roads which, since the building of the motorways, no longer carry much traffic; drive at a leisurely pace among the hills and valleys; stop now and again to unpack wine, cheese and olives in the shade of a tree; and look around. One can still find scenes exactly like those which provided Giotto, Perugino and Lorenzetti with settings for their great religious paintings. Where else could one find the motorised convenience of the present and the tranquil beauty of the past existing so harmoniously together?

That this guide covers Tuscany *and* Umbria, treating as one what are in fact two small, self-administering regions of central Italy, each independent of the other, is not without significance. Together they form the indivisible heart of Italy, and not only in a geographical sense. They are also, as the Austrian writer Adalbert Stifter once put it, 'a human place'. Not that this heartland of European culture is completely spared the blight of technological progress; far from it. On the plains surrounding the larger cities economic development has gathered pace, exploiting opportunities provided by access to international markets. The Tuscans in particular have rediscovered the spirit of enterprise which was the source of their greatness at the time of the medieval guilds. Inevitably this has involved losses. Year by year more of the idyll disappears as the effects of new technology are more widely felt. The authorities are careful however to preserve whatever can be preserved: the town centres, the beaches, the nature reserves, and the ancient Etruscan and Roman sites.

In the present century with its perhaps sometimes excessive passion for mobility, peoples become intermingled and regional characteristics may be discernible only with difficulty. Nevertheless it is still possible to meet the 'typical Tuscan' and the 'typical Umbrian'. The Tuscan is undemonstrative and uncomplicated, determined and matter-of-fact, in a friendly way. He tends to be slender, with fine face and pointed nose. The Umbrian on the other hand is altogether of heavier build, more relaxed, and more openly welcoming. Common to the people of both regions are an exceptional love of order and an untiring diligence, which do not, however, deprive them of an evident enjoyment of life.

Back-packing young travellers from all over the world have long since discovered that the dream of a different way of life is realised here in Tuscany and Umbria; they throng the ancient alleyways, adding colour — perhaps too much colour! But then it is part of the charm of today that there is no longer such a great divide between classes or incomes. The most important thing is to make up your own mind about where to go and what to see, and to know your way about well enough to do so.

Essential details in brief

Name: Repubblica Italiana (Republic of Italy).

Founded: The republic was established on June 2nd 1946. The constitution came into force on January 1st 1948.

Form of government: Parliamentary democracy, headed by the state president who is elected for seven years.
Parliament consists of two chambers, the 'Camera dei Deputati' (Chamber of Deputies) with about 600 members and the 'Senato della Repubblica' (Senate) with 350 members. The maximum duration of a parliament is five years.

Regional administration: Tuscany and Umbria are two of the twenty regions into which the Republic of Italy is divided. The Regional Statute of 1970 granted greater powers of self-administration to all the regions. They are responsible for tourism, traffic, agriculture and forestry, water and health.

Language: Italian.

Religion: Roman Catholic (97%), Protestant (c. 180,000) and Orthodox minorities, Jewish (35,000).

Population: About 57 million.

Pop. growth: About 0.4% per annum.

Capital: Rome (pop. 2.9 million).

Area: 301,263 sq km including Sardinia and Sicily.

Major exports: Machinery and motor vehicles; textiles and clothing; chemicals; agricultural produce (including vegetables, cheese, olive-oil, rice, fruit, wine and flowers).

Major imports: Oil, cars, chemical products, steel, agricultural products.

Major trade partners: West Germany, France, USA, Benelux countries, Britain, Switzerland, USSR, Austria, Japan, Brazil.

Other information: Among the organisations of which Italy is a member are the EC, UN, NATO, the OECD and the Council of Europe.

Life in Tuscany and Umbria

The most recent census (1981) showed the population of Tuscany and Umbria to be some 4.3 million. Tuscany is three times the size of Umbria with four times the number of inhabitants, and the smaller region has always been cast as 'poor relation' to the larger. Tuscany has a tradition of dynamism as a land of merchants and craftsmen, and a considerable amount of modern industry is already established there. Umbria, traditionally a land of farmers and saints where the pace of life was always more measured, is only now vigorously engaged in trying to catch up. Then again, Umbria, as the one region in the whole of the Italian peninsula which does not border on the sea, has only its hills, its mountains and a few wide river valleys; true, it does have a large lake, Lake Trasimene, but what is that, some would say, in comparison with the long sea coast of Tuscany with its lively ports like Livorno and Piombino?

Exodus from the land

During the period of Italy's industrial expansion in the fifties a great exodus from the countryside began. In Tuscany the movement was mainly from the land into the towns, from the hills down to the valleys and from inland to the coast. In Umbria however peasant farmers and shepherds left the region altogether, migrating to the industrial belt of northern Italy or even abroad. Of the two, Umbria had less potential for development. Tuscany, under Mussolini, had already acquired a motorway, albeit a relatively short stretch from Florence to the sea. As always Umbria found itself neglected, as it was at the end of the 19th c. with the building of the railway line to Rome. This linked Florence to the world but left Perugia, Umbria's major town, still isolated from the main transport routes. In Umbria only Orvieto looks down from its crag onto a mainline railway station with direct access to the international network, while Perugia acquired fast road connections no more than a few years ago. The Rome–Perugia and Florence–Perugia railway lines remain sleepy. But they offer the most delightful views of unspoilt countryside.

Above: The finished product
Left: The raw material

Tuscan farmhouse

Structural changes in the economy

How quickly the largely rural world of yesterday has been eroded, especially in Tuscany! Where once 40 per cent of its people were employed in agriculture now only 10 per cent remain; yet production has not declined. The mountainous areas and hilly tracts have been depopulated while the valley of the Arno, the Florentine basin and the coastal strip have become filled with people. Today 60 per cent are engaged in some form of trade, of whom a quarter are in commerce. This amounts to a complete structural change in the regional economy. Tuscany was formerly the region of *mezzadria*, a system of share farming which became established after the Middle Ages, when the rich from Florence, Pisa and Siena moved to estates in the country and ceased to be primarily bankers and wholesale merchants. Tenant families occupied smallholdings or *poderi*, administered by a central *fattoria*. They cleared the land and sowed and harvested the crops, paying the landowner half the yield. A family would occupy the same *poderi* for generations, thus giving the system great stability but at the same time dulling the entrepreneurial spirit on both sides. The system broke up very quickly after the last war as the rural exodus gathered pace and new laws were introduced favouring the smallholders. Many tenant farmers became owners of their land and agricultural co-operatives were set up to overcome the problem of small uneconomic holdings. Cultivation is now largely confined to areas where mechanisation is possible, with many economically less viable farms having been abandoned. The old and beautiful farmhouses have become holiday homes or second homes for city-dwellers from Florence, Rome and Milan, and for people from many other countries too.

Ten or more years ago something of a return to the land occurred with the increasing profitability of viticulture. This revival led eventually to the 'wine war' between Italy and France.

The changes that have taken place mean that these two small regions of central Italy are no longer quite the Arcadia they used to be, although much of the landscape of the 'rural paradise' is still there to be seen. Industry is centred primarily in the valley of the Arno, around Florence, Prato and Colle di Val d'Elsa, and along the coast between Carrara and Pisa. Here are concentrated the small businesses and craftsmen, the shoe and textile factories, the tanners, furniture manufacturers and metal-workers. Among the major industrial installations are blast furnaces in Piombino, Follonica, Livorno, S. Giovanni Valdarno, Florence, etc., engineering works, rolling-stock and shipbuilding yards in Livorno and Viareggio, tyre factories in Pontedera, makers of optical and precision instruments in Florence and a whole host of small chemical works, cement factories, and glass and

One of Assisi's many festivals

ceramics workshops scattered all over the place close to the towns. Though not of course comparable to anything quite as vast as the German Ruhr this part of Tuscany differs only in scale from other industrial regions in Europe.

Wholly unique, on the other hand, is Prato, the town which earns its living from the recycling of rags (see page 43). Away from the main industrial area Deruta is the traditional centre of the ceramics industry — though it often seems as if the whole of central Italy is engaged in turning the clay soil into either works of art or knick-knacks for the tourist trade. Perugia once led all its rivals in the manufacture of textiles for the fashion trade (a development pioneered by Luisa Spagnoli), but has long since ceded its position to Florence. Perugia is also the home of *baci*, little chocolate cakes with hazelnuts. Today this speciality is produced along with babyfoods by Perugina-Buitoni, a company formed from the merger of two old firms.

The good life — spas, wine and festivals
Tuscany has some of the strangest natural resources. At Larderello the *soffioni*, jets of hot steam rising from the ground, were first put to use by the Frenchman Larderell. Now they provide the heat source for four large geothermal power stations, a perfect example of clean energy. Clean hot water also flows from the many mineral springs at Montecatini, Chianciano and elsewhere, places which have long-established reputations as spas.

The wines of the region are famous, not just the Tuscan Chianti but also the wine from Orvieto in Umbria. Worth noting too is the trade in antiques. There are antique-fairs held all over the place (the best-known being in Florence and the rather more provincial one in Arezzo). Old furniture and utensils are on sale almost anywhere you go although, as the supply becomes exhausted, their place is gradually being taken by reproductions.

Folk festivals have come to assume increasing importance in the cultural life of the region. Prompted largely by the growth of tourism old traditions have been rediscovered and a deep pride has developed in them. Previously the festivals were considered relics of the old, wretched way of life and people wanted to be rid of them. Now their value as entertainment and a tourist attraction is fully exploited, and local patriotism has seen a great revival.

In late summer and autumn the roads of Umbria are lined with women and children selling mushrooms from overflowing baskets. Few of these mushrooms will be familiar to a visitor from outside Italy. But do have confidence in the expertise of the natives!

🐎 Signposts of history

Around 900 BC: Etruscan civilisation begins in Tuscany.

3rd c: The Romans consolidate their hold over Etruria. The consular roads are built, the Via Aurelia, Via Flaminia and Via Cassia.

217: Hannibal defeats the Romans at Lake Trasimene but the Etruscans remain loyal. Later there is a gradual deterioration of the coastal area and malaria spreads. Under Augustus the land is improved.

AD 317: Etruria (now referred to as *Tuscia*) amalgamated for administrative purposes with Umbria. The Roman Empire is in decline.

4th–8th c: The area falls successively under the rule of the Ostrogoths, the Byzantine Empire and the Lombards.

571: The Lombard duchy of Spoleto is established. (In the 8th c. it becomes part of the Frankish empire.)

752: Pepin the Short becomes king of the Franks after presenting 23 towns to the Pope (Pepin's Donation).

917: Gubbio is destroyed by the Huns.

1077: The Emperor Henry IV journeys to the castle of the Margravine Matilda at Canossa for his meeting with Pope Gregory VII.

1116: The new military power Pisa is victorious over the Arabs and Saracens, a milestone for Christianity in the fight against Islam.

1155: Barbarossa destroys Spoleto. Umbria remains the battleground between Holy Roman Empire and papacy.

12th–13th c: The power struggle between emperor and pope continues, with each finding supporters among the rising city states. Florence in particular suffers from internal feuding but eventually becomes the strongest city loyal to the papacy.

1182–1226: The Franciscan religious order is established by Francis of Assisi.

1215: The first university is founded in Arezzo.

13th–14th c: Dante Alighieri, Petrarch, Boccaccio, Cimabue and Giotto create their masterpieces.

1348: The Black Death ravages central Italy.

1389–1464: The rule of the Medici begins with Cosimo the Elder.

1449–1492: During the lifetime of Lorenzo the Magnificent Florence and Tuscany become the centre of Renaissance humanism and culture.

1498: The Dominican monk Savonarola is executed. Machiavelli, Leonardo da Vinci, Michelangelo and Raphael work in Florence and Rome in the decades around the turn of the century.

1531: The Emperor Charles V captures Florence and establishes the duchy of Tuscany, bringing to an end the Florentine city state. The Medici return to Florence with Charles's support and become grand dukes.

1540: Perugia finally falls to the papal forces and is destroyed, losing its independent status.

1737: The last of the Medici princes dies. Tuscany passes to Francis of Lorraine, husband of the Habsburg Empress Maria Theresa.

1808–1815: First Tuscany and then Umbria (1809) are annexed by Napoleon. Following this interlude Tuscany once again comes under the control of the House of Lorraine, and the Papal States re-establish their rule over Umbria.

1860: The *Risorgimento* brings Tuscany and Umbria together in a united Italy.

1865–1870: For a time until Rome capitulates (1870) Florence is capital of Italy. With the annexation of the Papal States Rome finally becomes the capital again.

Castellina in Chianti

 Phases of history

Etruscans and Romans

Etruscan culture can be identified in Tuscany from about 900 BC onwards and in a relatively short space of time a kind of Etruscan 'state' became established. The Umbrians, a people who had earlier migrated from the north into the upper valley of the Tiber, adjusted to this presence by largely adopting the Etruscan way of life. Arezzo, Chiusi, Cortona, Vetulonia, Volterra, Gubbio, Spoleto, Terni, Todi and Perugia were small towns in the Etruscan mould. Of these only Perugia was numbered among the Twelve Cities, the confederation through which over a long period the Etruscans defended themselves against the advancing Romans. Eventually, however, they were all of them brought under Roman control, with the aid of strongholds built along the cross-country routes, the Via Flaminia and the Via Cassia.

After the collapse of the Roman Empire the two regions came successively under the rule of the Ostrogoths, Byzantium, and the Lombards. Their shared history ended in the 8th c. when the Lombard empire was absorbed into the Frankish, and the Lombard duchy of Tuscany became a Frankish margraviate. Umbria was handed over to the Papal States by Pepin and Charlemagne. It was not until a thousand years later that the two regions were brought together again, with the unification of Italy. The Frankish-German margraviate of Tuscany (under the Margravine Matilda) played an important part in the conflict between Holy Roman Empire and papacy. The meeting between Emperor Henry IV and Pope Gregory VII took place in 1077 at Canossa, seat of the Margravine's family.

Throughout the 11th c. Pisa was developing into a military and political power. Pisan victories over the Arabs and Saracens (1116) were milestones in the struggle of Christianity against Islam. Increasingly aware of its growing economic might the city emancipated itself from episcopal rule, while the building of Pisa Cathedral was also begun.

In the 12th c. the neighbouring city of Lucca, former capital of the old Lombard duchy of Tuscany, came to dominate the European trade in woollens and silks, establishing a monopoly in terms of trading with the towns of Lombardy and those north of the Alps. At Siena the great expansion of the city in the 12th and 13th c. was founded upon the wealth of the big banking houses (Buonsignori and Salimbeni).

Conflict between Guelphs and Ghibellines

Florence however came to dominate all the other cities of Tuscany, steadily growing in economic, political and cultural importance. The conflict in the 12th and 13th c. between the Guelphs and the Hohenstaufen dynasty, rival German claimants to the Holy Roman Empire, persisted in Italy as a struggle for power between the papacy and the empire, the 'Guelphs' being those on the papal side and the 'Ghibellines' those supporting the emperor. The loyalties of the Tuscan cities varied. Pisa and Siena were both Ghibelline. In Florence internal strife was eventually resolved in favour of the Guelphs and the city emerged as the most powerful of the forces loyal to the pope. The Florentine banking houses (Bardi and Peruzzi) flourished.

This period also saw the first heyday of Tuscan culture. In 1215 the first university was founded in Arezzo, Pisa and Siena following a century later. The Tuscan dialect became the language of Italian literature through the writings of Dante Alighieri (1265–1312), Petrarch (1304–74) and Boccaccio (1313–75), whose lyrical *dolce stil' nuovo* became the dominant poetic style. The painters Cimabue (c. 1240–1302) and Giotto (1266–1337) hastened the transition from Byzantine and Gothic to Renaissance art.

Politically the period was a ferment of troubles: between the Guelphs and the Ghibellines, between the nobility and the middle class, between the guilds and the labourers. A revolt begun by the *Ciompi*, the wool-carders, for instance, was only put down months later through the concerted efforts of a number of important families. One such was that of the Medici, a banking family who became the dominant force in the city. In the 15th c. Cosimo the Elder (1389–1464) and in particular his grandson Lorenzo the Magnificent (1440–92) made Florence and Tuscany the centre of Renaissance culture and humanism. Under Lorenzo's son Piero (1471–1503), however, the city was unable to hold out against the French king Charles VIII when he invaded Italy, and Piero was banished into exile. For a short time the crusading fervour of the Dominican monk Savonarola attracted an influential following but in 1498 he was condemned as a heretic and executed. The age of Florence the great city state was drawing to a close. In 1531 the Emperor Charles V seized Florence and established the duchy of Tuscany (from which however Lucca was excluded). Yet even in these decades of political decline the city experienced a new intellectual flowering: Niccolò Machiavelli (1469–1527) set down the principles of statecraft in *The Prince*, drawing on his experience as statesman and diplomat; Leonardo da Vinci (1452–1519), Michelangelo (1475–1564) and Raphael (1483–1520) employed their great talents in the service of numerous princes and popes.

Tuscany — model possession of the Habsburg Empire

The Medici returned to Florence as dukes (and later grand dukes) of Tuscany after Charles V had nominated Alessandro de' Medici head of state, the dynasty eventually dying out in 1737. The grand duchy passed to Francis of Lorraine, husband of Maria Theresa, and then into the possession of the emperors of Austria. Tuscany became a model of the Habsburg conception of enlightened absolutism. Torture and the death sentence were abolished (for the first time in Europe), government was re-formed, and the drainage of the marshes of the Maremma and the Chiana valley was improved. The Napoleonic conquest and subsequent resumption of Austro-Lorraine rule were no more than interludes before the unification of Italy by Cavour and Garibaldi. In 1865 Florence even became the capital of Italy for a time, until 1870 when the Papal States were annexed and Rome assumed its rightful role.

Umbria in the shadows of Tuscany and the Papal States

The development of Umbria was shaped by its proximity to Rome. To begin with the Byzantines still had ready access to Perugia, Terni and Narni through the 'corridor' provided by the valley of the Tiber, but they were barred by the Lombard duchy of Spoleto to the east of Terni. Not until the time of the Hohenstaufens did Umbria become the link between the Papal States and their possessions on the Adriatic coast. It was also in the 12th c. that the Umbrian towns of Perugia, Assisi, Foligno, Spoleto, Terni, Todi, Orvieto, Gubbio and Città di Castello succeeded in establishing themselves as city states. Spoleto was brought to its knees by Frederick Barbarossa and Perugia acquired a position of regional supremacy.

Umbria's position is assured above all in the history of religious movements. During the period of Ostrogothic rule Benedict of Nursia (Norcia) had already become the founder of Western monasticism. In the 12th c. Francis of Assisi (1182–1226) established the Franciscan order, making Umbria one of the religious centres of Europe. Jacopone da Todi's devout hymns, the *Laudi*, and the frescos by Cimabue and Giotto at Assisi also sprang from this all-embracing piety, while the flagellant movement originated in Perugia.

From the early 14th c. Perugia became an important university city. In Foligno in 1472 Dante's *Divine Comedy* appeared in print for the first time, while the Umbrian school of painting reached its zenith in the work of Benozzo Gozzoli (1420–97) and Perugino (Pietro Vannucci, 1448–1523). In 1540 Perugia was taken by papal troops and deprived of its status as an autonomous city. The region sank into a sort of torpor. Without the stimulus of free economic and cultural rivalry between the towns and lacking any direct access to the coast it reverted to being a backwater. Regional autonomy was restored after the collapse of the Papal States. It is only in recent decades that industrialisation has gradually begun to alter the pattern of Umbrian life.

Fontana Maggiore, Perugia

Cinerary urn from the Etruscan Museum, Volterra

 # For the art-lover
Etruscan culture

It is not known whether the Etruscans were an indigenous tribe or migrants from elsewhere in the Mediterranean. What is certain is that, from about the 9th c. BC, they colonised the area between the Tyrrhenian coast and the banks of the rivers Arno and Tiber. Their lively art, which strangely enough is best known to us from their tombs, is immensely pleasing. Though unquestionably influenced by the Greeks it remains more naive, not striving in quite the same way for Classical perfection. The Etruscans were good farmers, resourceful traders and excellent craftsmen, and in view of their highly developed forges and elaborate bronze castings they might even be described as an industrial people. The area of present-day Piombino was a sort of ancient Ruhr, exploiting iron from the island of Elba. They had an outstanding urban culture, achieving a high degree of refinement. Today the cities they founded often still bear the names of two and a half millennia ago — Faesule (Fiesole), Saena (Siena) and Perusia (Perugia) among others. They

Assisi, home town of St Francis

13th c. mosaic from the baptistry, Florence

exercised a cultural influence over the conquering Romans. By the Middle Ages however their tombs had been plundered and the elaborate gold, silver and bronze artefacts scattered around the world. Today museums in Volterra, Siena, Arezzo, Cortona, Chiusi, Florence and elsewhere all house some Etruscan art, though none have the wealth of exhibits that Rome and Tarquinia possess. New treasures are still coming to light, like the gigantic figures discovered at Talamone in 1982.

The city states — cradles of the arts

It was not until the 13th and 14th c. that Tuscany and Umbria once again developed an artistic life of their own, correspondent with the emergent civic vitality of the autonomous city states. Pisa had its own distinctive style of architecture (cathedral, baptistry, church of S. Paolo a Ripa), the influence of which can be seen in Prato and Pistoia as well as in the great cathedrals of the coastal towns as far north as Carrara. The cities vied with one another architecturally, Lucca, for instance, building in its own enriched Romanesque style (cathedral of S. Martino, church of S. Michele). There are also unusual variations in the secular architecture, for example in the often fortress-like and turreted *palazzi* — the council buildings and the residences of the ruling families, *priori* (guildmasters) or *podestà* (chief magistrates). Familiar with the superb architecture of Lombardy, the sculptor Nicola Pisano introduced, with his son Giovanni, a new vitality into the depiction of religious scenes. In Lucca and Pisa inspiration also came from the 'discovery' of the huge painted crucifixes (by Guglielmo — c. 1138 — Buonaventura Berlinghieri, Coppo di Marcovaldo and others). By the end of the 14th c. the dramatic and monumental figures of the painter Cimabue had come to define the style of painting of central Italy as a whole, soon even in Siena where, since the 13th c., the Madonnas of the Byzantine-Gothic school had been characterised by an extraordinary tenderness (Duccio di Buoninsegna).

'Imported' Gothic

Gothic was first introduced in the monastery buildings of the French Cistercians (S. Galgano at Siena, S. Salvatore near Florence) and became fused with the native Romanesque style. Italian Gothic differs from northern Gothic, being rather less audacious, and each city adapted it in its own way. In Florence, where examples include the churches of S. Croce (by Arnolfo di Cambio) and S. Maria Novella as well as the first phase of the cathedral, the Gothic strives for a colourful, geometrically ordered splendour, very evident in the cathedral campanile designed by Giotto. Painting too responded to this northern influence. In Siena Simone Martini imported the elegance of 'international Gothic' from Avignon which was then the seat of the papal court. At the same time the brothers Pietro and Ambrogio Lorenzetti seized upon Giotto's revolutionary use of light and dark contours and unified space — the beginnings of perspective. Giotto was the first painter to 'tell a story'.

Siena and Florence influenced each other, and this resulted in a mutual enrichment which in turn spread to other cities including Perugia, Pisa and Orvieto. At the beginning of the 15th c. — the Early Renaissance period — Florence acquired its position of unchallenged cultural supremacy. The Florentine architectural tradition, always Classical in tendency, evolved further with the tightly controlled but at the same time light management of space created by Filippo Brunelleschi (1377–1446), who had studied Classical architecture in Rome. Now anything 'Gothic', by which was meant anything 'dark' or 'barbaric', was banished. Informed by a new self-consciousness and spirit of individualism and with a new confidence in man's role as master of the world — derived in large part from the rediscovery of the achievements and ideals of Classical antiquity (renaissance means rebirth) — architects now proclaimed, in their churches and palaces, the arrival of a different art. It was secular and humanist, no longer piously mystical and other-worldly. This new consciousness radiated outwards from Florence transforming the arts and sciences across the whole of central and western Europe.

Tuscany — heartland of the Renaissance

The Early Renaissance — to about 1500 — reached its zenith in Florence, the High Renaissance — to about 1600 — in Rome.

Brunelleschi's influence dominated Florentine architecture for almost a century. During this period S. Lorenzo, S. Spirito, the Pazzi Chapel and many other great building projects were completed, including the city's most glorious landmark, the mighty dome which rises over the cathedral. In sculpture Lorenzo Ghiberti's bronze doors to the baptistry provided the stimulus for a new creativity. Donatello's was the supreme talent, but from their *botteghe* numerous masters like Luca della Robbia, Antonio del Pollaiuolo, Andrea del Verrocchio and Jacopo della Quercia, aided by dozens of assistants, made their contributions to the splendour of Florence.

In painting the discovery of perspective represented the greatest innovation. At the same time, the ideal after which all the painters strove, the faithful representation of a perfect human image in a perfect space, found its own unmistakable form of expression in the work of each of the great artists. During his short life (1401–28) the earliest of them, Masaccio, was responsible for the austere, powerful frescos in the Brancacci Chapel (S. Carmine in Florence). In contrast, the frescos by Masolino, Masaccio's older friend who was also his collaborator on the chapel, are painted in a less decisive, softer style, while Filippino Lippi in his continuation of Masaccio's work added a distinctive quality of gracefulness.

Michelangelo Buonarroti

Art thrived during the brilliant period of the Medici but suffered with every political and economic crisis, war and epidemic. These swings of fortune are well illustrated by the career of the long-lived Michelangelo (1475–1564). He began by familiarising himself with the paintings of Giotto and Masaccio, was apprenticed to Ghirlandaio, and studied the Classical statues in the Medici gardens of S. Marco (the art school of the time). Yet he was also a contemporary of the revolutionary zealot Savonarola who consigned to the flames any art he deemed too secular and who even caused Botticelli to renounce his earlier more worldly style. Michelangelo lived through the fall of the Medici, but also witnessed their return. Having to work sometimes in Florence, sometimes in Rome, he undertook commissions from no fewer than six popes, three of whom came from the Medici dynasty. The young Raphael (1483–1520) also moved to Rome. Florence was no longer the undisputed epicentre of Renaissance art, but it had by then attained its own perfection.

Flora and fauna

The flora of both Tuscany and Umbria has been shaped to a large extent by man. The typical scenery with its olive-groves is in reality 'artificial' since the olive-tree is not native to Italy. It was brought from Asia Minor during Antiquity and transplanted there. The vine on the other hand is indigenous; even the Ausonians, the original inhabitants of Italy who were there long before the Romans, cultivated it. *Ausonia* (land of vines), the poetic name for Italy, is still used, especially on wine labels.

Primavera *by Botticelli*

Of the forests which formerly clothed the Apennine peninsula only sparse remnants now survive. The evergreen Mediterranean macchia, the impenetrable scrub that once covered the Tuscan coast, has likewise receded or been cleared. What still remains of it can best be seen in the Maremma and on the Argentario peninsula: stone-pines, dwarf oaks, cork- and holm-oaks, strawberry trees, erica (the height of a man), myrtle, dwarf palms and broom. Sweet-chestnut trees flourish even at 1,000 m above sea-level. Flour made from ground chestnuts was at one time an important food for the poorer farmers, just as acorns were a staple feed for their pigs. In the hills around the monasteries of Vallombrosa and Camaldoli, tracts of pine forest have been preserved and replanted.

Few of the original species of fauna have been able to survive the Italian passion for hunting, nor have the deer introduced later fared any better. It is said that one or two wolves do still survive in the Umbrian mountains. The thousands of weekend hunters insist that there are foxes and hares, but usually only a few thrushes are to be seen hanging from their game-bags. So it is encouraging to find that even in Italy the younger generation is more interested in nature conservation than hunting and the hunting laws are now somewhat stricter. The slaughter of songbirds on a massive scale has certainly cost the Italians much in the way of public sympathy. Nowadays at any rate, when *uccelli e polenta* features on the menu, it is almost certainly made from specially reared quail rather than songbirds.

✕ Food and drink

The art of cooking faces a dilemma that faces every art today: 'specialities' are fast disappearing because class and other differences are disappearing. These days everybody eats everything. But true specialities do still exist, meat for instance in Tuscany and fungi (truffles) in Umbria.

Eating in an Italian restaurant means having a full meal, that is to say at least a *piatto primo* (first course) and *piatto secondo* (second course), though more and more the Italians themselves are turning away from such substantial fare (not least because prices have become quite steep).

Nevertheless it is still not customary to order only a plate of spaghetti. Waiters will not be insulted though if the secondo chosen is just a salad, a vegetable dish or cheese. Another possibility is to order only a *mezza porzione* (half portion) of the first course and to indulge oneself with the second, which as a rule consists of meat or fish. For dessert people often just eat fresh fruit, although many restaurants are well known precisely for their delicious *dolci*, their sweet dishes. In the towns the cafés offer the alternative of an abundance of tasty snacks including every variety of pizza, ice-cream sundaes, sandwiches and toast. In the country you can explain to the proprietor that you simply want a *spuntino*, a light meal of bread, ham, salami and cheese, served with wine and olives.

Over and above the price of the meal you must reckon to pay the usual *pane e coperto* or bread and basic cover charge, as well as a service charge of 15 per cent. And on top of that the customer is expected to leave a further tip of 5 to 10 per cent.

Lunch is usually between 12.30 and 3 pm. In the evening the restaurants open at the earliest at 7.30 pm although at that time the chefs and waiters are often having their own meal. Things get going properly at around 8 pm and continue late into the night.

Starters

Friò is a Tuscan speciality of late summer: thick slices of potato and onion flavoured with basil and strong spices, steamed and then cooled in the *frigo* (refrigerator) and eaten cold. It is served with *carne lessa* (boiled meat), also eaten cold — *gallina lessa* (boiled chicken) for example, or *lingua lessa* (tongue).

Insalata is simply salad (our word derives from it), and literally translated means 'salted'. *Insalata mista* is mixed salad, *di campo* is flavoured with wild herbs, and *insalata di finocchio* is fennel salad. Cold spinach and other vegetables are also eaten *all'agro* (that is, with a little vinegar and oil) as an accompaniment to the main dish.

Soups

Minestra is a vegetable soup, the simplest variety being called *minestrone*. Other soups have their own particular names. The familiar kind of tomato soup is *crema di pomodoro* (sieved and thickened soups in general being *crema*). Meat soup is called *brodo* but with a beaten egg added it becomes *stracciatella*.

Ribollita is a Tuscan soup *à la maison*: haricot beans with paper-thin slices of onion and a great deal of olive-oil. It owes its name (*ribollita* meaning boiled or reboiled) to the length of time taken in the cooking and to the fact that it used to be made from leftovers, a practice scorned in Italy. *Acqua cotta* — literally 'boiled water' — is another dish from the *cucina povera*, the poor man's table.

Caciucco alla Livornese is a soup made from fish, squid and mussels in pulped tomato, cooked with sage and oil and served with slices of garlic toast. (Incidentally, cheese should never be sprinkled on fish soup!)

Zuppa di frutti di mare is similar to *caciucco alla Livornese* but made with such delicacies as mussels, crab and lobster.

Entrées

Salsice are thick, rather coarse pork sausages brought crisp to the table in the frying pan (*in padella*) or from the grill (*alla griglia*).

Polpette are simply meat balls to which grated Parmesan cheese and chopped mushrooms are added; they are usually stewed in tomato sauce.

Fagioli — haricot beans removed from the pod — appear on every menu in Tuscany and Umbria. *Fagioli all'uccelletto* are first boiled and then cooked in pulped tomato with sage and pepper. They are eaten hot or cold or as a vegetable side-dish.

Frittata is basically an omelette, with herbs, vegetables, bacon and sometimes also potatoes mixed in or as a filling. Sweet omelettes are an imported dish and are called by the somewhat superior name *crêpe*.

Tortino is also a kind of omelette. It is similar to *frittata* but much thicker and the vegetables — artichokes *(carciofi)* and onions for example — are mixed into it before it is fried.

Local produce for sale

Boleti, flat mushrooms, still grow wild in great abundance in Umbria. They are prepared differently from elsewhere, the stalks being removed and a small clove of garlic pushed into the cap before they are grilled.

Meat dishes

Bistecca fiorentina: an enormous T-bone steak — easily enough for two!

Bistecca milanese: Wiener schnitzel; *bistecca alla parmigiana:* Parmesan cheese schnitzel.

Arrosto di maiale: roast pork; *arrosto di vitello:* roast lamb.

Manzo: beef; *pollo:* chicken; *agnello:* young lamb; *capretto:* kid; *abacchio:* lamb.

Fegatelli di maiale: small pieces of pig's liver wrapped in laurel leaves and fried, usually highly flavoured with garlic and fennel seeds.

Agnello alla cacciatora: lamb *à la chasseur* (however odd that sounds, since lambs are not exactly hunted!). In practice *alla cacciatora* simply means that the meat (other types too, e.g. chicken) is chopped into pieces and braised in pulped tomato with herbs.

Capriolo: roe deer *in umido* — well hung and stewed in wine with a spicy sauce.

Pappardelle alla lepre: ragout of hare served with noodles.

Pasticcio: layers of *lasagne* with a hare filling, baked in the oven.

Fagiano dei bosconi: a Tuscan speciality, but nowadays the pheasants are more likely to be bred than from the wild (*bosconi* — woods). The bird is roasted in olive-oil, well seasoned and trimmed with bacon slices.

Desserts

Formaggio pecorino (ewe's milk cheese) *piccante* or *dolce* — strong or mild — is served after the meal.

Panforte di Siena: very sweet, highly spiced, close-textured cake made with candied fruit and whole almonds.

Castagnaccio is the traditional dessert: a dry cake made from chestnut-flour with nuts, raisins, pine-kernels, olive-oil and a lot of sugar. It is only for strong stomachs.

Cenci which can be bought at any baker's are similar to doughnuts and fried in oil.

Frutta (fruit): for the Italians an irresistible end to the meal. It means fresh fruit, but sometimes *frutta cotta* (compote) also appears on the menu.

Coffee and breakfast

Espresso, the universally familiar thimbleful of black elixir, is not so called because it is brewed quickly but rather because every little cup is individually prepared 'expressly for each person'. In fact the longer it takes to go through the espresso machine the better it is. If you want it served with a little milk ask for a *macchiato;* a *cappuccino* is a medium-sized cup. The closest to what we are used to is a *caffè latte*. Popular at breakfast is a glass of (hot or cold) milk with a dash of espresso *(latte macchiato)* or, in colder weather, a dash of brandy *(latte al cognac)*. The usual breakfast *cornetti* (horn-shaped pastries) and a kind of superior *brioche* are served at the stand-up counters in cafés and bars. Cakes are called *dolci*, and if you want to take them away with you *(portare via)* the cashier will put them in a small bag.

Two typical recipes from Tuscany

Braised wild boar

For 6 people: Put 1 onion, 1 carrot, a large stick of celery and 3 sprigs of fresh rosemary in slightly less than a cup of olive-oil and heat. When the oil begins to sizzle add 2 kilos of wild boar meat cut into large pieces (ordinary pork may also be used). Leave to braise, then remove the rosemary, season with salt and pepper, flavour with garlic cloves pressed with the grated peel of a lemon and add a fresh sprig of rosemary. Continue braising, adding a glass of dry white wine. Wait until the wine has been absorbed then leave to simmer in a light stock or water. Finally stir in two tablespoons of skinned tomatoes, but without letting them cook for long. The whole thing is an exercise in patience, taking a good two hours!

Baked haricot beans

Leave a good amount of the small Tuscan haricot beans to soak overnight. Heat at least a quarter of a litre of pure olive-oil in a clay oven-dish (of the kind sold in Tuscany at every weekend market), adding a small bunch of all the herbs available as well as celery, carrot, onion and the soaked beans. Season with salt and pepper and cook in a pre-heated oven until the beans have soaked up the oil. Remove the herbs. This meal is so nourishing that meat is superfluous.

... and of course Chianti

This is pronounced 'kianti' and the wine has both its history and its problems. Production costs have soared. Ten years ago 10,000 kg of Chianti grapes would have paid for a tractor; today 30,000 kg would not be enough. It is the same story with the price of chemical fertilisers. Wages too are high, and yet there is still a shortage of labour.

Chianti vineyards are only legally denominated as such when certain varieties of grape are cultivated: 50 to 80 per cent *Sangiovese*, 10 to 30 per cent *Trebbiano toscano* and *Malvasia di Chianti*, and 10 to 30 per cent *Canaiolo*. The dry, full-bodied blend of red wine was first produced 150 years ago by Baron Ricasoli at his castle *Brolio* (still the best-known Chianti). The officially recognised area of Chianti production is in the hills around Florence, Siena, Pisa, Montalbano and Rufina.

Chianti vines, Anghiari

Chianti classico is identified by the black cockerel or *gallo nero* on the label. There are some 730 Gallo producers, who have formed themselves into a consortium. The Chianti marked with the *putto* (cherub) is not quite as *classico*. There is a legend about how the black cockerel came to feature on the coat of arms, a legend that still angers the Siena vintners. During the Middle Ages at the time of the numerous feuds between the cities of Florence and Siena, a halt was called to hostilities in 1208. A method was agreed for defining the boundary between them. Two riders were to leave Florence at first cock-crow, and two riders were likewise to leave Siena. The boundary was to be established where they met. The sly Florentines starved their cock of food the day before, so that it started to crow long before dawn. The riders from Siena had only got as far as Fonterutoli when they met their rivals, having of course lost a lot of ground.

The preferred policy today is to limit production in order to maintain prices (and quality). The Italians no longer drink as much wine as they used to, not so much on grounds of abstinence but rather because they have discovered beer and other drinks. France is still Italy's best customer for wine, though also its keenest competitor; in the United Kingdom, for example, people still tend to buy French wines despite the relatively low prices of the wines from Italy.

On the terraced slopes of the Chianti region there are already signs of change. Where once everything was hoed by hand small tractors now clatter, and the vines are supported by concrete posts instead of wooden stakes. How long can the classic Tuscan landscape survive? The agricultural mandarins demand a reduction in wine output, and suggest growing raspberries and hazelnuts instead! But any such change would have to be financed by the public purse, and the public purse is empty. So people hesitate to get rid of the vines. The Tuscans produce about 7 million tonnes of grapes a year, that is, 4.7 million hectolitres of wine. Of this total, however, only 1.2 million hectolitres qualify for the DOC label (Denominazione di Origine Controllata) guaranteeing its origin.

Festivals

The Florentine festivals apart, Siena heads the festivals list with its world-famous *Palio di Siena* (see page 82).

At Arezzo a jousting tournament, the *Giostra del Saracino*, is held on the Piazza Grande. Eight riders, each representing one of the city's districts, charge at the wooden effigy of a Saracen. The rider who strikes closest to the centre of the Saracen's shield wins the 'golden lance'. A historical pageant precedes the jousting. This festival goes back to 1593; it was forgotten for a century and then revived some sixty years ago.

In Pisa a regatta called the *Regata storica di S. Ranieri* is held on the Arno (nowadays, sad to say, somewhat polluted), and the *Gioco del Ponte*, the traditional 'battle' on the Ponte di Mezzo, is fought out between two teams. At Sansepolcro there is a crossbow tournament, the *Palio della Balestra*, and in Lucca a religious festival, the *Festa della S. Croce*. The Italians get enormous fun from the *Carnevale di Viareggio* with its huge procession of carnival floats, a main theme of which is political caricature.

Foremost in Umbria are the religious festivals and pilgrimages, especially those at Assisi (see page 68), Cascia (see page 78), and Gubbio (see page 63). Foligno stages a *Giostra della Quintana*. In Orvieto the Corpus Christi festival is one of the highlights of the year, as too is the extraordinary Whitsun dove festival, the *Festa della Palombella*, when the descent of the Holy Spirit is commemorated in the piazza outside the cathedral with a ceremony involving a white (mechanical) dove and an explosive finale.

Almost all the smaller towns have found something to celebrate in one way or another, be it a donkey race or an artichoke festival. These are advertised locally with banners and posters. In Perugia the *Città della Domenica*, a children's amusement park, is open throughout the year.

A different sort of entertainment altogether is offered by the cultural festivals: Spoleto's *Festival dei Due Mondi*, the *Maggio fiorentino* in Florence, the Music Weeks (*Sagra umbra*) at Perugia, and the *Cantiere* in Montepulciano.

On horseback in the Maremma

No one in Italy knows more about horses than the Maremma *buttero*, a local equivalent of the cowboy. Since early this century (with the draining of the malarial marshes) a special breed of horses has been raised here. There are about thirty studs, the best-known belonging to Countess Ponticelli alla Trappola, near the seaside resort of Principina a Mare. Pony-trekking across country following specially created bridleways through the dense macchia (scrub) can be arranged through Montefreddi (tel. 055/813 433, 222 232) or Rendola Riding (tel. 055/987 045) in Florence, Le Cannelle (tel. 0 564/887 020) in Grosseto, and Rifugio Prategiano (tel. 0 566/997 703) in Montieri.

One itinerary, Arezzo–Pienza–Arcidosso–Saturnia, treks practically the whole way round Monte Amiata. Another, lasting six days, starts in Capocavallo di Corciano (Perugia) and — with a break at Lake Trasimene — takes riders via Siena and San Gimignano to the Tyrrhenian coast. This is anything but a cheap form of leisure activity, however.

Giostra del Saracino, Arezzo

H Thermal spas

Tuscany is planning to develop its thermal spas into one of its major attractions in the future. Montecatini Terme, at the foot of the Apennines (45 km from Florence) was already well patronised under the Austrian dukes of Tuscany. The waters and steam from eight mineral springs offer relief for sufferers from liver and intestinal complaints. The little town, built in the style of the turn of the century, has a great many hotels of every category (as well as family-run pensions).

Chianciano Terme, a very much smaller, rather homely spa, is reached from Siena or, more easily still, from Chiusi. Four mineral springs provide treatment for heart trouble and stress. It is a very suitable place for convalescence, the pretty surroundings and the fashion shops helping to boost patients' morale. The little spas at Sarteano and S. Casciano dei Bagni, not far from Chianciano Terme, are more rural in their setting. The Romans long ago put their faith in the forty-two springs at S. Casciano dei Bagni. Saturnia, easily reached (55 km) from Orbetello or Grosseto via Manciano, is the place for anyone seeking to take the waters in the grand style. The hydro is sited in the valley away from the town, beside a hot sulphur lake fed by a mighty underground spring (1,000 litres of sulphurous water per second, at a temperature of 37.5°C). It is definitely worth taking a swim in the warm (blood-temperature) lake, if not for health reasons then just for pleasure. Medical supervision is available and the cuisine and wines are of the best. The surrounding countryside is still completely unspoilt and there are Etruscan necropolises and early medieval remains not far away at Sovana and Sorano; worth seeing also is Pitigliano perched high on a rocky spur (cathedral, Palazzo Orsini).

Does it bite? Shopping in Florence

 # Shopping

No holiday will ever stay within budget unless a certain amount is included from the start to cover souvenirs and presents. Nor would the little craft businesses survive very long if the tourist were not tempted into spending money on modern or traditional items like gold and silver jewellery and gemstones (some real, some not). There are other articles worked every bit as delightfully: ceramics, lace and embroideries, exquisite handbags and shoes, baskets, mats, hats, lampshades, wineglasses — and of course the wine to drink from them.

Ceramics make a suitable souvenir for almost anyone. There is something to fit every purse: the cheapest figurines, the most expensive decorative plates painted with Classical patterns, bowls, pots, tiles — the finest art and the most delightful knick-knacks. The best-known town for ceramics is Deruta (on the main Perugia-Terni road); it has been famous since 1387. The *Museo della Ceramica* there has a magnificent permanent collection as well as holding a design exhibition every three years. Although items are on sale in the exhibition rooms, near the petrol station, it is well worth visiting the lovely old town itself where there is one shop after another. It only remains to add that while Deruta is the cradle of ceramic art, the potter's craft is at home in all the other towns of Umbria as well.

Wrought-iron work has always been special to Gubbio, as has another very singular local craft — making wooden crossbows — which are on sale in many tiny shops. Indeed one of the best-known of all the festivals is the annual crossbow tournament, the *Palio della Balestra* (see page 64). People with a lot of money to spend can take home crossbows elaborately decorated with intarsia; but nowadays the traditional art of wood inlay is also applied to useful things like trays, pretty wooden boxes and small pieces of reproduction furniture.

Art prints and art books — old or second-hand — are among the best buys in Tuscany and Umbria. Such prints and illustrated volumes can be found at any newspaper kiosk. The largest selection is in Florence at Alinari (a firm now 130 years old which pioneered many photographic and reproduction techniques).

Look or ask at the second-hand bookstalls for *I Maestri del Colore*, published by Fratelli Fabbri (perhaps the most comprehensive illustrated series covering the great Italian painters). Excellent reproduction and remarkably cheap!

Hints for your holiday

Carabiniere: symbol of Florence

In the height of the tourist season the real Italy is not so easy to track down, especially in the major cities. If holiday plans allow try to wait until the crowds of sightseers have left in their cars and coaches before making your own excursion — it is evening before the Italians themselves fill the piazzas and corsos. Strolling along with an ice-cream and gazing around, or enjoying a leisurely supper outside a trattoria in the piazza, it is possible for a while to share their sense of belonging. Young people perch together on the rim of a fountain or gather in groups on the steps of the old churches; men stand around in the cafés talking heatedly about football; and in the alleyways women bring chairs to their doors and sit chatting, plying their needles.

A good rule of thumb for visiting churches is 'the earlier the better'. The best time to look round a church is as soon as possible after morning mass (though don't of course disturb the service). Not only is the light generally favourable at that hour in the morning but nowadays many of the smaller churches are only opened for services, the priests no longer being able to afford any staff. Most churches stay closed during the lunch break (12 noon–3 pm). Tourists by the way are expected not to visit places of worship in shorts, or bare-shouldered. At many of the best-known churches, in Assisi, Perugia and Florence for example, attendants posted at the entrance will turn away anyone unsuitably dressed.

It is equally advisable to make an early start when visiting museums, especially the major ones. They are always very crowded.

Maremma Nature Park

Where to go and what to see

The coast of Tuscany

Prime attraction for holidaymakers in Tuscany is undoubtedly the sea, several hundred kilometres of mainland and island shoreline on the long Tyrrhenian coast, with sand and rock, pine woods and macchia, all waiting to be enjoyed. Every sort of waterborne activity is catered for, sailing, windsurfing, motor-boating (including hire), or just paddling about having fun on one of those *mosconi* (pedalos). You can play boccia on the beach, go riding, play tennis or golf, take lots of walks or simply laze around.

The Apuan Riviera, just south of the port of La Spezia, is the start of the traditional bathing resorts where a century ago the formerly water-shy Italians first braved the surf. Here it was that the Macchiaioli, landscape artists who followed in the steps of the French Impressionists, painted their delightful beach pictures of pretty ladies under parasols, and fishermen's huts and boats set against the unending blue horizon. Today's holidaymaker benefits from the Riviera's long-established seaside tradition. The beaches themselves are not heavily built up, each town being situated a little way inland with only its marina offshoot actually by the sea. Away from the coast rise the impressive Apuan Alps, the marble of the mountains at Carrara providing an unusual and majestic backdrop. The rewards of an excursion into this still relatively undisturbed hinterland should not be missed once the pleasures of the beach have been enjoyed to the full.

The Apuan Riviera

Between Marina di Carrara and Viareggio an unbroken chain of hotels extends along the coast through Marina di Massa, Cinquale, Forte dei Marmi, Marina di Pietrasanta and Lido di Camaiore, forming to all intents and purposes a single holiday resort. Excursions are easily undertaken no matter which resort you choose, by coach from Marina di Massa for example to the famous marble quarries (Forno, Renara, Valsora), or up to the Carrara alpine refuge high in the mountains (1,320 m above sea-level). Not far from Forte dei Marmi is Seravezza (beautiful cathedral) with a quarry from which in 1517 Michelangelo selected snow-white marble for the papal tomb he was working on in Rome. Other routes lead to Pietrasanta (cathedral of S. Martino, Palazzo Moroni, Palazzo Pretorio, and a permanent exhibition of marble-working). At Camaiore there is a Romanesque church, *La Collegiata*, and also a Roman-esque abbey nearby.

Cavallino Bianco, 138 Via Lorenzi, Camaiore (tel. 0 584/913 672).

Versilia

Viareggio Pop. 58,500

Viareggio is the main seaside resort on the stretch of the coast known as Versilia. The town was originally established by the city of Lucca, which hostilities between Pisa, Genoa and Florence deprived (in 1440) of any other access to the sea. Viareggio still has lovely forests of stone-pines, and a lively and picturesque harbour with numerous fish restaurants. More inter-esting to some people than the cele-brated Viareggio carnival will be the town's premier cultural events, including the presentation of the *Premio Viareggio* — Italy's foremost prize for literature — and the associated summer concerts.

Nightclub in Viareggio

Fedi da Gianfranco, 111 Via Verdi (tel. 0 584/48 519); *Foscolo*, 79 Via Ugo Foscolo (tel. 0 584/44 220); *Da Pino*, 18 Via Matteoti (tel. 0 584/43 356); *Tito del Molo*, 3 Lungomare C. del Greco (tel. 0 584/962 016).

The Pisan coast

Marina di Pisa is surrounded by macchia, large tracts of which happily still survive — the Macchia di Migliarino, Macchia di S. Rossore and Macchia di Tombolo. These merge with the Lucca Macchia and are being combined into a single nature reserve. Broom, holm-oaks, black pines and stone-pines, strawberry trees, myrtle and giant erica are all intermixed, often in an impenetrable tangle, like a jungle. The *Tenuta di S. Rossore* (3,000 ha), once the hunting grounds of the Medici and later owned by the Italian royal family, is now owned by the state and serves as the president's summer residence. It is open to visitors on Sundays and public holidays only.

The hotels and campsites along this uniformly flat and sandy stretch of coast, which is partly fringed with dunes *(tombolo)*, provide every kind of facility for a beach holiday. There is tennis, riding, sailing, windsurfing and a multitude of other sporting activities.

The Etruscan Riviera
Livorno Pop. 176,300

Livorno (Leghorn) is Tuscany's large and busy principal port. Apart from the bastions

Livorno

of the old harbour and the later fortifications built by the Medici dukes there is not really a great deal of interest to the tourist. The seafood however is very good. There are bathing beaches at Ardenza and Antignano to the south of the city (hotels and camping).

 Accademia, 16 Via Lepanto (tel. 0 586/806 198); *La Barcarola*, 63 Viale Carducci (tel. 0 586/402 367); *Oscar a Ardenza*, 78 Via Franchini (tel. 0 586/501 258).

Beyond Livorno the mountains close in on the sea and the picturesque stretch of coast known as the Etruscan Riviera begins. Situated in dense pine woods are the resorts of Quercianella and, further south, the elegant Castiglioncello.

The Maremma

At Cecina Mare begins the northern Maremma which extends southwards as far as the Piombino promontory. Here where the mountains once again recede from the coast the land was first drained by the Etruscans but later allowed to revert to a malaria-infested swamp. Today this part of the coast is actually healthier than most others since it is still only sparsely populated and quite unpolluted by industry. Near S. Vincenzo there is the Rimigliano nature reserve, which has a campsite tucked away in its furthest corner at Torraccia (room for 500 people). Beyond that the coastline opens out into the unspoilt Golfo di Baratti, in Etruscan times the harbour for the town of Populonia (Etruscan tombs).

Piombino is the ferry port for Elba. After suffering destruction in the last war it has recovered to become a lively town. Anyone heading for the southern Maremma di Grosseto however can leave Piombino to the right and follow the road through Follonica (a busy little industrial town) to a new seaside holiday mecca, fashioned out of two bays forming the northern shore of the headland at Punta Ala. Here the mountains once again press in close to the coast and in places the pine woods come right down to the sea. Punta Ala is a luxury beach resort, well furnished with large hotels, villas and campsites. Despite the distance (220 km) it serves as a pleasure ground for the capital, Rome. Inland the province of Grosseto has developed into a vast agricultural area. No trace now remains of the *Maremma amara*, the once neglected, wretched, disease-ridden Maremma.

The chain of bathing resorts stretching from the small town of Castiglione della Pescaia in the north to Orbetello in the south is broken between Principina a Mare and Talamone by the exceedingly beautiful Maremma Nature Park in the *Monti dell'Uccellina*.

From there it is not far to the Laguna di Orbetello. A narrow causeway crosses the *laguna* (lagoon) to the rocky promontory of Monte Argentario with its little harbours of Porto S. Stefano (ferry to the Isola del Giglio) and Port'Ercole. The modern-day Romans have assiduously colonised Monte Argentario, building villas on the rocky but lush macchia-covered slopes. Local prices are geared to them, as they are also in the small beach resort of Ansedonia, on the mainland. Not far from there the nature reserve at *Lago di Burano*, where the lake is a paradise for birds, lies close to Tuscany's southern border with Lazio.

 La Casareccia, 202 Via Senese, Grosseto (tel. 0 564/451 470); *La Pagoda*, Hotel Gallia Palace, Punta Ala (tel. 0 564/922 022); *Egisto*, 190 Corso Italia, Orbetello (tel. 0 564/867 469); *La Formica*, Località Pozzarello, Porto S. Stefano (tel. 0 564/814 205); *Il Gatto e la Volpe*, Via dei Cannoni, Port'Ercole (tel. 0 564/833 306).

Porto Azzurro, Elba

The Tuscan islands

The islands off the Tuscan coast are a world of their own. Elba, a favourite especially for German holidaymakers (and villa-owners) is now completely opened up. All its towns and resorts have good services connecting them with the harbour at Portoferraio, and all are well provided with restaurants, particularly seafood restaurants as you would expect. The island is extremely busy in summer but a haven of peace out of season. It is a paradise for sailing and underwater sports.

The Isola del Giglio and the smaller, less well known island of Giannutri (ferries from Porto S. Stefano) have managed to preserve an air of unspoilt remoteness. Traces left here by the ancient Romans show that they must have appreciated it too (Giannutri: Villa Romana).

The land of the Etruscans

On the way home by car from a beach holiday a delightful route of discovery awaits anyone who would still like to learn something about the mysterious world of the Etruscans. This is anything but a museum tour; it is the stark landscape itself, well inland from the coast, which has its ancient history. The Etruscans (see page 10) settled here 900 years before the birth of Christ. They were industrious farmers, and a laughter-loving people with a great enjoyment of life, as can still be divined from their tombs. The country around Monte Amiata has perhaps not changed very much since those days. Follow the SS 1 (Via Aurelia) for a short distance from Orbetello as far as Albinia before turning off to the right onto the Manciano road (the SS 74). This takes you up into the so-called 'old Maremma', the high-lying part of the formerly extensive Maremma swamplands: here in their little towns the people were safe from malaria. From Manciano there is a side-road (easily found) which soon leads to the village of Montemerano and on to Saturnia, the famous spa with its hot spring.

After that detour continue along the SS 74 to the small town of Pitigliano, curiously perched high on an elongated crag. From here another road branches off to nearby Sorano. Anyone seriously on

the trail of the Etruscans will also want to follow the signs to the necropolis at Sovana (quite an experience for people making the excursion on foot).

Rejoin (beyond Sorano) the section of the SS 74 abandoned earlier to go in search of the Etruscans, and continue to the junction with the SS 489. Now head for Lake Bolsena. For a short while the road runs close to the border with the neighbouring region of Lazio. Enjoy the view of the lake before taking the SS 71 to nearby Orvieto and its Etruscan necropolis — directly in front of the town, half-way up the tuff crag on which Orvieto stands (see page 79). From there the journey home can be resumed.

Da Michele, Piazza Vittorio Veneto, Saturnia (tel. 0 564/601 074); *Taverna Etrusca*, Piazza Pretorio, Sovana di Sorano (tel. 0 564/616 183).

The harbour at Port'Ercole

View over Florence

Florence and the north

Driving from Florence to Pisa along the arc which passes through Prato, Pistoia and Lucca leaves the visitor with a myriad of impressions; it is a memorable journey, distinguished less by the beauty of the scenery than by the magnificence of the urban architecture. The Florentine basin, the foot of the Apennines around Prato, the Ombrone valley at Pistoia, the delightful *Lucchesia* around Lucca and the coastal plain at Pisa are the most densely populated areas in Tuscany. Year by year they become more heavily industrialised, as the dense network of roads and the heavy traffic testify.

What really brings the landscape of this area alive is remembering that in the Middle Ages each of the cities was an autonomous entity, and that over these distances, now telescoped by modern life, the city states — Florence and Pisa in particular — fought relentless wars one against the other. It is to their rampant civic pride that we owe the buildings, the sculpture and the paintings, an extraordinary heritage created as the rivals sought to surpass one another in greatness. Not until later were the cities joined in common alliance.

Florence Pop. 450,000

It would take a lifetime to really get to know Florence. So the best plan will be to fill in a few background details and then to focus on the most important things to see. Longer-stay visitors in search of more extensive information should refer to a guide dealing specifically with the city.

Florence was not only the most resplendent city of the Middle Ages, it was also the most culturally fertile. Here it was that so much of what is characteristic of our modern age had its source, in the growth of popular representation or democracy, in the guilds and the banking houses, and in the spirit of humanism and scientific enquiry, the art and architecture of the Renaissance.

For centuries the history of Florence has alternated between periods of splendour and periods of calamity (see page 11). But again and again the city has shown itself possessed of the strength to re-create and to revive, most recently after the great flood in 1966. Today the face of Florence is perhaps more lovely and 'youthful' than ever before. The city has preserved its treasures, renovated and restored them, and now lives off them. Of course with its industrial suburbs, regional government, university and institutes, fashion houses and congress halls it is a thriving economic centre as well. But while Florence is no tourist island like Venice neither is it burdened with world politics like Rome.

 Exploring Florence

Pedestrian precincts provide today's art-

orientated visitor with the opportunity for peaceful contemplation. Florence has thus succeeded in harmonising its thriving commercial life with its historic heritage of buildings and art treasures.

A first city walk

Piazza della Signoria: Start at this glorious square in which for 1,000 years Florentine history has been made. When it was first built in the 13th and 14th c. older squares of houses were pulled down to make way for the Palazzo dei Priori, as the *Palazzo Vecchio* was then called. This was the residence of the ruling *priori*, guildmasters, and the *gonfalonieri* (generals). The bold building with its slender 94-m-high tower was once also known as the Palazzo del Popolo — the people them-

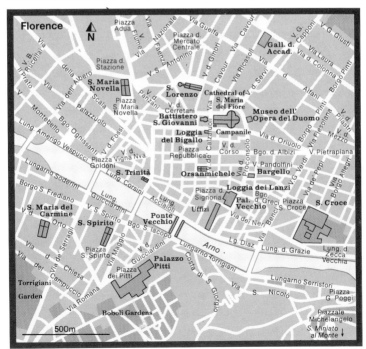

A copy of Michelangelo's David *(left) and Ammanati's fountain (right) in the Piazza della Signoria*

selves were in control for a time. The point of the tower bears the emblems of the city, a lily and a lion. Until 1400, for their entire period of office the priori and the gonfalonieri were obliged to take up residence together, living and sleeping on the second floor and guarded by 100 soldiers. The Council of One Hundred, the Upper House, met on the first floor while the Civic Council of 300 representatives held its meetings on the ground floor. Of the interior rooms the Hall of the Five Hundred (1495) is especially worth visiting (though it should be said that democracy at the time — under the Medici — was strictly for appearances). It was at the first sitting held in the hall that Savonarola delivered his inflammatory address, inveighing against excessive worldliness and grandiose living. Later on he was condemned and was first hanged and then burnt at the stake in the square (a stone set in the pavement 10 m from the fountain commemorates the event). The hall

now serves as a venue for concerts.

On the piazza are a copy of Michelangelo's *David* (the original of 1504 is in the Accademia), Donatello's *Lion*, Giambologna's equestrian statue of Grand Duke Cosimo I (1594) and Ammanati's *Neptune Fountain* (1575). To the right of the Palazzo Vecchio is the *Loggia dei Lanzi* where Cosimo I's German mercenaries were once quartered and their horses stabled. There are important statues by Cellini and Giambologna to be admired.

Orsanmichele, in the Via Calzaiuoli near to the Piazza della Signoria, is a Late Gothic building, beautifully preserved and richly decorated inside and out. It was once a corn exchange (one of the channels through which grain was delivered from the granary above can still be seen in the right-hand corner). Belief in the miraculous

Right: Palazzo Vecchio

qualities of an image of the Virgin Mary led to the building becoming a place of pilgrimage, and the guilds eventually converted it into a church. The figures in the niches on the exterior are by Verrocchio, Donatello, Lamberti and Giambologna, while the darkly mysterious interior contains a tabernacle by Andrea Orcagna and an altarpiece by Bernardo Daddi.

Bargello

Botticelli's Birth of Venus in the Uffizi

other side of the Arno. The Palazzo Pitti later became the seat of government but the Uffizi still contains Italy's largest art gallery. On her return to Florence the last Medici heiress Anna Maria Lodovica, widow of Düsseldorf's legendary Jan Wellem, made a gift to the city of the huge collection she had preserved for it. Originally, the top storey of the building immediately beneath the roof was living-quarters and workshops for the craftsmen kept by the Medici family. It was there, in conditions almost amounting to slavery, that they cut every one of the 100,000 stones used in the Chapel of the Princes in S. Lorenzo. In 1585 a theatre was constructed in which the first opera was performed. Even in those days the arcades of the Uffizi's long wings were occupied by shops, as they are now.

The Uffizi: Adjoining the *Palazzo Vecchio* (which over the years has been repeatedly added to and extended) is the end of one wing of the Uffizi. This long building was originally offices for the Tuscan state administration, but even then an upper storey was earmarked for a gallery to house the Medici art collection. Started in 1560 to plans by Giorgio Vasari the Uffizi was enlarged during its many years under construction and is even connected via the Ponte Vecchio to the *Palazzo Pitti* on the

Bargello: The sheer size of the Medici art collection led eventually to its being split up. As a result the sculptures, gold- and silver-work and even some of the paintings are now in the Bargello Museum (Via del Proconsole, two minutes' walk from the Piazza della Signoria). Once the residence of the city's chief of police (*bargello*), the massive building, with prison cells where members of the rebellious Pazzi family were held awaiting execution, is a typical

A royal apartment, Pitti Palace

Pavilion in the Boboli Gardens

Florentine fortress with tower and enormous courtyard.

Ponte Vecchio: Next cross the Ponte Vecchio, the only bridge not blown up in the last war. It is now a delightful shopping street, especially enchanting in the evening when the lights sparkle in the gold- and silver-smiths' windows. At its midpoint look down from the open parapet of the bridge into the dark waters of the Arno, in flood a continuing threat to the venerable old bridge and the Old Town. From here it is only a short walk through narrow, bustling streets to the *Palazzo Pitti.* A morning visit to the Pitti Gallery and a walk in the *Boboli Gardens* on the slopes of the hill behind convey better than anything the splendour of the later period of rule by the long-surviving Medici family.

A special tip

For a glimpse of the cultural life of contemporary Florence visit the Art Nouveau *Caffè* in the Piazza Pitti, a meeting place for actors, producers and musicians.

Ponte Vecchio

S. Spirito: Designed by Brunelleschi S. Spirito (Piazza S. Spirito, a couple of steps from the Ponte Vecchio) is the classic Renaissance church. Although the architect did not live to see it finished and later modifications were made, Brunelleschi's basic vision was preserved by those who came after him (including Manetti, Giuliano da Sangallo and Antonio Pollaiuolo). They added sacristies, a campanile and cloisters to this prodigious building. In the interior the strict arrangement of columns and vaulting is further emphasised by the economy of colour — brick red and stone grey. With this church European art recaptured the spirit of Antiquity and put the Middle Ages to flight.

S. Maria del Carmine (Piazza del Carmine) reveals by its exterior little of the treasure to be found within. The place of the *Brancacci Chapel* in the history of art is still secure, its frescos by Masaccio and Masolino having survived a devastating fire undamaged. The chapel can properly claim to be the 'cradle of European painting'. Masaccio began work on it in 1423, collaborating with his compatriot Masolino, who was almost twenty years his senior. Masaccio never saw the chapel completed, however; at the age of twenty-seven he disappeared in Rome, probably a victim of the plague. He was responsible for the scenes *The Expulsion of Adam and Eve* and *The Tribute Money*; *The Fall* and other scenes are the work of Masolino. The chapel was later completed by Filippino Lippi. (Good light during the morning. Closed for restoration from 1989.)

A second city walk

The *Battistero S. Giovanni* (baptistry), the massive *Duomo S. Maria del Fiore*, the elaborate *campanile*, the *cathedral museum*, the *archbishop's palace* and a row of medieval buildings (*Loggia del*

The cathedral façade

Bigallo and *Misericordia)* crowd together on a square so confining that sadly no single view can encompass them all.

Cathedral of S. Maria del Fiore: In 1296 the citizens of Florence decided to replace the old church of S. Reparata with a new cathedral. It was to take its name from the city (Fiorenza) and was therefore called *S. Maria del Fiore*; it was also to be a focus for civic pride — at the time power was concentrated in the hands of the monastery churches of S. Maria Novella, S. Trinità and S. Croce. Initially Arnolfo di Cambio was in charge of building but after his death Giotto took over. Construction — to which the citizens themselves contributed energetically — was repeatedly interrupted by unrest and epidemics. Not until 1412 was the façade erected and work begun on the vaulting for the dome. It was then that Filippo Brunelleschi set to work on his inspired solution to the problem of the dome, pioneering the way for future architecture. His design involved

Around the cathedral

two domes, the weight of the outer one being carried by a strong inner framework beneath. But Brunelleschi died before its completion and it was 1467 before the cathedral was ready to be consecrated. The present façade dates from only 1875 when it was rebuilt in a style harmonising with the campanile. The cathedral interior, 153 m long with a transept 90 m wide, is beautiful in its simplicity. What the centuries have added in the way of ornamentation has either since been removed or is concealed in the sheer spaciousness. Of special interest (left aisle) are the twin equestrian fresco portraits of two *condottieri*, John Hawkwood painted by Paolo Uccello (1436) and Niccolò Manuzi da Tolentino by Andrea del Castagno (1456). In the *Museo dell'Opera del Duomo* (9 Piazza del Duomo) is a late work by Michelangelo, a *Pietà* intended for his own grave. It was broken in pieces by the artist and later (1559) reconstructed by Cavalcanti. There are also important works by Donatello, Ghiberti, Luca della Robbia

The campanile

The Battistero S. Giovanni

and others, some of which have been brought here to avoid further weathering.

The campanile like the cathedral itself took an interminable time to build. Following Giotto's death the execution of his design was continued first by Andrea Pisano and later by Francesco Talenti, though it was never fully completed. Even so there is nothing in the least 'unfinished' about this unique building, faced with coloured marble and richly ornamented with figures. It stands in inspiring testimony to the genius of its creators who sought to capture a whole world of belief and ideas in their imagery. The reliefs by Andrea Pisano and his pupils include scenes from the Bible and allegories of the natural sciences.

The Battistero S. Giovanni opposite the cathedral façade is almost certainly built on the site of a Roman Temple of Mars. The foundation stone of the present church was laid in 1060, construction commencing in 1128. In time the church came to be surrounded by tall tombstones, which have since been removed. The octagonal building has always held a powerful fascination for Florentine artists.

In 1330 Andrea Pisano began work on the oldest of the baptistry's famous bronze doors (south side), depicting the story of St John the Baptist. Later Pisano's reliefs were enclosed within a superb bronze frame by Ghiberti (assisted by Pollaiuolo, Botticelli and others). Ghiberti's own masterpiece is the exquisite east door, decorated with scenes from the Old Testament. The sculptor and his assistants worked on it for over twenty years. It is this door which Michelangelo christened the Door of Paradise because of its perfection.

In spite of its very precise geometry the interior of the baptistry has an unexpected spaciousness and mystic quality, stemming from the softly glinting mosaic ceiling with its gigantic figure of Christ at the Last Judgement.

S. Maria Novella (next to the main railway station) rewards a visit with superb frescos by Ghirlandaio, Filippino Lippi, Nardo di

The cloisters, S. Maria Novella

S. Lorenzo

Cione (in the Strozzi Chapel) and Masaccio. The latter's famous fresco of the *Trinity* (c. 1425) is one of the seminal works of the Renaissance. Adjoining the large Gothic church which originally belonged to the Dominicans are cloisters known as the *Chiostro Verde* and a refectory with yet more delightful frescos.

S. Lorenzo (by Brunelleschi), 'chapel royal' of the Medici whose palazzo stands nearby (not far from the Piazza del Duomo), is like a pattern book of architectural style from Early Renaissance to Baroque. Donatello and Michelangelo contributed to it. There is complete harmony in the articulation of space and arrangement of the sculptures; everything is ordered by a strict geometry. The façade of the church is still in rough brick, surviving testimony to a painful chapter in Michelangelo's life: his original commission was withdrawn, and instead he was employed to complete the *new sacristy* as a burial chapel for the Medici family. Before that was finished, however, he was summoned to Rome, and the chapel and

the *Biblioteca Laurenziana* which he also designed had to be completed by others. The play of forms between the vestibule, doorway, staircases, false niches and pilasters has fascinated later architects.

A third city walk

The large square in front of the church of *S. Croce* (not far from the north bank of the Arno near the Ponte delle Grazie) is the start of a third area of great historic interest.

S. Croce, a lovely early mendicant church, possesses without any question one of the jewels of the Renaissance, the *Pazzi Chapel* in the First Cloister. The Pazzi commissioned Brunelleschi to build a suitably magnificent family burial chapel. There are a number of similarities with the baptistry but the chapel interior is unusually light, not at all sombre or other-worldly. The terracotta medallions and tondo figures are the work of Luca della Robbia.

The Second Cloister, also designed by Brunelleschi, leads to the *Canigani Chapel*

S. Croce

Pazzi Chapel, S. Croce

and the old *refectory* which is now the *S. Croce Museum*. On the end wall of the refectory is a superb fresco of the Last Supper by Taddeo Gaddi. Everything here deserves to be enjoyed quietly and at leisure.

A special tip

Still in S. Croce a room off the passage which runs from the monastery church to the cloister is now a workshop belonging to the association of Florentine leather-workers. Another room has been turned into a shop where you can buy attractive leather boxes stamped with the lily emblem, including luxury versions with expensive gold decoration. The range of prices is wide, though, and people on a limited budget are equally well catered for, with purses, wallets, bookmarks and book covers, spectacle cases, bowls, etc.

S. Miniato al Monte: To round off your sightseeing make the climb (via the Piazza Michelangelo and Viale Galilei) to the church of S. Miniato al Monte. It is well worth the effort, especially at sunset for a fine view of Florence with its domes and towers. Not only the church but all the buildings of the Olivetan monastery are a tribute to the greatness and persistence of the Tuscan spirit. The origins of the building can be traced back to AD 250 when Minias, a Christian, was beheaded on the orders of the Roman emperor — the church probably stands over his tomb. Interminably long phases of construction followed, continuing till 1800. The typically patterned façade with facings in white and green rises resplendent above the wide steps and the cemetery — and above the surrounding gardens which, with their fine trees, provide a wonderfully impressive setting for viewing the great city astride the banks of the Arno.

Maggio fiorentino.

 Sabatini, 9a Via Panzani (tel. 055/282 802); *Buca Lapi*, 1 Via del Trebbio (tel. 055/213 768); *Leo in Santa Croce*, 7r Via Torta (tel. 055/210 829); *Osteria Numero 1*, 22 Via del Moro (tel. 055/284 897); *Enoteca Pinchiorri*, 87 Via Ghibellina (tel. 055/242 777); *Le Fonticine*, 79 Via Nazionale (tel. 055/282 106); *Osteria 1. Rosso*, 1 Via Borgognisanto (tel. 055/284 897); *13 Gobbi*, 9 Via del Porcellana (tel. 055/298 769); *Burde*, 6 Via Pistoiese (tel. 055/3 170 206).

Ex Excursion to Fiesole

Fiesole (founded by the Etruscans) is situated on a hill overlooking Florence. The *cathedral* was built between the 11th and 13th c. Walk round the *Zona Archeologica* — there is a Roman amphitheatre and a museum with Etruscan and Roman finds. On the way back to Florence go on foot at least as far as *S. Domenico*; at *Badia Fiesolana* there is an abbey with a Renaissance church. The journey by trolley-bus is quite an experience too! Behind the typically high walls along the very narrow roads olive-groves and lovely old villas can be glimpsed.

Roman amphitheatre, Fiesole

The cathedral, Prato

From Florence it is only about 25 km to Prato on the A 11 or the SS 66 (Pistoiese).

Prato Pop. 162,000

Even those who drive past, intent on a visit to its more illustrious neighbour Florence, will find it impossible to 'overlook' Prato. The town's very stable textile industry provides its inhabitants with a unique way of earning a living, recycling rags and other textile waste from America and Europe. The waste is turned into the finest exportable materials ranging from artificial leather and plush to luxury fabrics, spun and woven 'from old into new' in hundreds of businesses, small, medium-sized and large. It all started with cast-off clothes sent from the USA after the war. From this a wonderfully resilient system of mutually supporting enterprises has developed, protected from even the worst crises by diversification at every level. Even farmers on the edge of town have electronically controlled looms.

What to see

Palazzo Pretorio: Prato's ancient heritage can only be discovered by first fighting your way through the bustling suburbs to the Palazzo Pretorio (on the Piazza Comune, in the Old Town) with its interesting *Galleria Comunale*, and from there across the Via Manzoni to the *Piazza del Duomo*.

The cathedral with its striped façade in light-coloured and dark green stone is famous for its *Pergamo del Sacro Cingolo*, an outside pulpit by Donatello and Michelozzo. The outer wall of the pulpit is adorned with Donatello's delightful dancing *putti* (cherubs), one of the loveliest pieces of Renaissance sculpture. The interior of the cathedral is sombre and severe. Its many chapels include the *Cappella del Sacro Cingolo*, decorated by Agnolo Gaddi among others. The frescos tell the story of the *Sacro Cingolo*, the Virgin Mary's girdle, which was brought here from the Holy Land. The statue of the *Madonna and Child* (c. 1317) and the *Crucifix* (in the main nave, on the right) are masterpieces by Giovanni Pisano. A small courtyard leads to the *Museo dell'Opera del Duomo* which contains some important paintings and the original reliefs from the external pulpit (these can be viewed at eye-level), as well as remains of the old cloister.

Palazzo Datini: Right at the very heart of the town on the corner of Via Ser Lapo Mazzei is the Palazzo Datini, now the public record office, richly emblazoned with coats of arms. It was the residence of Francesco di Marco Datini, Prato's most renowned merchant banker (1330–1410), who entertained his many august

contemporaries there. The *Datini Archive* accumulated by this financier to the popes has been preserved intact. Dating from the time of the papacy's exile in Avignon it now represents an immensely important source of historical information. In his day Francesco Datini was also a notable social benefactor as the monument to him testifies. He founded *Il Ceppo dei Poveri*, an early charity for impoverished woolcarders.

S. Francesco: On the *Piazza S. Francesco* there is an Early Renaissance church of the same name. Like the cathedral it has a façade of alternating green and white stripes; there is also a cloister and chapterhouse. Inside the church is Francesco Datini's tomb.

Castello dell'Imperatore: On the left beyond S. Francesco, beside the *Piazza S. Maria delle Carceri*, stands Frederick II's mighty Hohenstaufen castle. It is the only one of its kind in the whole of central Italy, and reminiscent of the Castel del Monte in Apulia. The imposing Renaissance church of *S. Maria delle Carceri* was begun by Giuliano da Sangallo but not completed until after his death.

Museo d'Arte Contemporanea Luigi Pecci: This museum of modern art built by Italo Gamberini was opened in 1988.

 Il Piraña, 110 Via Valentini (tel. 0 574/25 746).

Leave Prato by the SS 64 and a drive of some 20 km along a flat stretch of road brings you to Pistoia. The city lies at the north-western end of the Ombrone valley which runs southwards towards the Arno.

Pistoia Pop. 92,000

Pistoia is a busy place, industrial and commercial. Only by forsaking the comfort of your car and making your way on foot can you penetrate the city's innermost sanctum, the *Piazza del Duomo* with its surrounding medieval buildings.

Around the cathedral

There is a long history attached to the lovely *cathedral* with its terracotta decoration by Andrea della Robbia. The 67-m-high campanile was originally a Lombard watch-tower to which a further three storeys of loggias were added in the 14th c. Opposite the cathedral is the Gothic *battistero* designed by Andrea Pisano, and to its right is the austere 14th c. *Palazzo del Podestà* or *Pretorio* (now the courthouse). Facing this is the *Palazzo del Comune*, a forbidding sandstone building begun by a Florentine podestà, Giano della Bella, in 1294 — though not completed for a long time. In the piazza the characteristic *pozzo* (well-head) in the north-east corner is the work of Cecchino di Giorgio and dates from 1453. Beyond the *Ospedale del Ceppo* (the old poorhouse — *ceppo* means stump, on which alms were placed) with its frieze of majolica reliefs, the Via del Ceppo leads first to Michelozzo's church of *Santa Maria delle Grazie* (15th c.) and then by way of the Via Buonfanti to *S. Bartolomeo in Pantano*, a 12th c. church built as the name implies (*pantano* = marsh) on swampy

ground. The Via S. Pietro leads from the cathedral square to the former church of *S. Pietro Maggiore*.

Other sights

But Pistoia still has more to offer. Starting from the *Palazzo Pretorio*, go down the narrow Via degli Orafi and on past the church of the *Madonna dell'Umiltà* to the bishop's palace. The *Diocesan Museum* there has some important 14th and 15th c. paintings.

For anyone whose appetite is even then still unsatisfied there is yet more fine architecture to be seen: the impressive church of *S. Andrea* with a beautiful pulpit by Giovanni Pisano, the very large *S. Francesco*, its splendid *chapter-house* newly restored, and the church of *S. Giovanni Fuorcivitas* which has a fine pulpit of its own.

 Rafanelli, 47 Via S. Agostino (tel. 0 573/23 046).

From Pistoia much the best plan is to take the Firenze—Mare motorway (A 11). It is rich in lovely views, especially of the gently undulating hills and the fortresses of Valdinievole near Montecatini Terme. However, while the SS 66 (Pistoiese) — joining the SS 435 (Lucchese) — is a more twisting road, it too leads to the plain at the foot of Monte Pisano, and to Lucca.

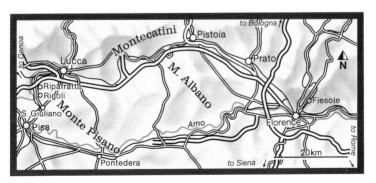

Lucca Pop. 90,000

Lucca is a town it would be a joy to live in. Large enough to be full of life but without being overcrowded, it lies at the foot of mountains yet within easy reach of the sea. Greatest of all its attractions however is its medieval architecture, preserved virtually intact, with only the addition of one or two Renaissance buildings and a little Baroque.

All new building has been banished outside the gates and kept a respectful distance from the ramparts. These mighty bastions splendidly planted with trees form a popular and at times populous round walk taking about an hour to complete. But there is no harm at all in taking longer over it: there could be no more pleasant introduction to the buildings encircled within.

  The town centre

The heart of the town is the *Piazza Napoleone*, the name a reminder of Napoleon's gift of Lucca to his sister Eliza (the square is also known as the *Piazza Grande*). She did not retain possession for long and the town eventually became part of the duchy of Tuscany under the Habsburg Duke Leopold. The real history of Lucca, however, is to be discovered in its medieval buildings.

Cathedral of S. Martino: The *duomo* was founded as early as the 7th c. and rebuilt in the 11th c. by the future Pope Alexander II. It was completed in its present form only in the 14th c. Chief among the many fine sculptures in the interior is the famous and very moving *tomb of Ilaria del Carretto* (the young second wife of a nobleman, Paolo Guinigi, ruler of Lucca). Her marble resting-place (1408) is the work of the sculptor Jacopo della Quercia. *Putti* and heavy garlands of flowers adorn the frieze around the sarcophagus on which, with eyes closed, the serenely beautiful figure lies enfolded in her gown. At her feet is a little dog.

Case dei Guinigi: Further on from the cathedral (Via Guinigi) are the *Case dei*

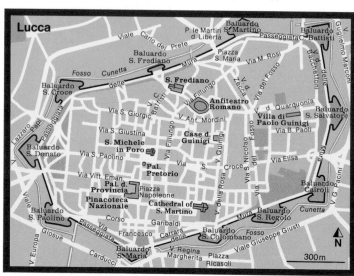

Cathedral of S. Martino

S. Michele in Foro

Guinigi, a compact complex of palace buildings, the best example of Lucca's Romanesque architecture. The great tower, on top of which holm-oaks grow, can be climbed.

Churches

Of the many churches *S. Michele in Foro* — not far from the *Palazzo Pretorio* (on the site of the Roman forum) — and, in particular, *S. Frediano* — reached by way of the Via Cesare Battisti — should not be missed. Although S. Frediano was built in the 12th c. it incorporates some remains of an earlier church, a fact to which a font inside, the *Fontana Lustrale*, bears witness. The *Cappella Trenta* (1413, left-hand aisle) contains sculptures by Jacopo della Quercia.

From S. Frediano the Via Fillungo leads to the *Anfiteatro Romano*, a most unusual circular market place surrounded by houses which are now being gradually restored. The original amphitheatre was treated as a convenient quarry, providing materials for Lucca's marble churches — an example of the unfettered destruction suffered by so much art.

Museums

For those who enjoy museums and have the time to indulge themselves the *Pinacoteca Nazionale* in the *Palazzo Mansi* (Via Galli Tassi) has a collection of paintings dating from the High Renaissance to the 19th c. They were presented to Lucca in 1847 by Duke Leopold II when the town was incorporated into Tuscany — and what a gift! The *Villa di Paolo Guinigi* (Via della Quarquonia) has been the home of the *Museo Nazionale* for some years now; its collection includes paintings, furniture, and relics of the town's history.

Festa della Santa Croce (mid-September).

Da Giulio in Pelleria, 29 Via S. Tommaso (tel. 0 583/55 948); *Il Giglio*, 2 Piazza del Giglio (tel. 0 583/44 058).

From Lucca head east along the old Via Pisana, with the River Serchio on one side and Monte Pisano on the other, to the small spa of S. Giuliano Terme, passing on the way the pretty little town of Ripafratta with its medieval towers and the villages of Rigoli and Corliano. Then continue the journey to Pisa along the SS 12.

Pisa Pop. 104,000

There is far more to Pisa than its leaning tower. To see the city properly will take at least a full day — preferably not in the height of summer! Of course all paths lead first to the *Campo dei Miracoli* (translated literally 'the field of miracles') where the cathedral, the baptistry, the leaning tower and the great cemetery are set among the lawns of the Campo — an architectural ensemble famous the world over.

What to see

Cathedral of S. Maria: The *duomo* is a masterpiece of Romanesque architecture, a style which Pisa was to develop in a form all its own. Begun in 1064 by Buscheto the building was consecrated while still unfinished in 1118. The *façade* is by the architect and sculptor Rainaldo.

Despite its construction having been spread over such a long period, the massive cathedral still presents an overall harmony. Look for example at the Late Renaissance bronze doors and then at the Romanesque *Porta S. Ranieri* in the transept! The interior of the five-aisled church is beautifully light, with a three-aisled transept and imposing dome vaulting. On the left is the celebrated *pulpit* (*pergamo*, 1302–11) by Giovanni Pisano, the supreme example of Italian Gothic sculpture, decorated with vigorously dramatic scenes of the life and sufferings of Christ. From the ceiling hangs the *bronze lamp* whose swinging is said to have led Galileo Galilei, then at the University of Pisa, to the discovery of the law governing the motion of the pendulum. Over the centuries the cathedral has been further embellished with frescos, paintings and mosaics. In the *Sagrestia dei Cappellani* (on the right) is the *tesoro del duomo*, the treasury.

The campanile: The cathedral campanile —the Leaning Tower or *Torre Pendente*—

Campo dei Miracoli – the baptistry, the cathedral and the Leaning Tower

must surely be the world's most famous bell-tower. There cannot be many people who are entirely unaware of its unique statistics. It inclines to the south at an angle of about five and a half degrees. The average deviation from the vertical is 2.25 m but between the first and seventh galleries the deviation is greater (2.95 m). It is now known that the tower was not deliberately built at an angle as was once commonly believed; on the contrary the ground subsided after building had begun (1147). When work was resumed above the third gallery after a pause of about 100 years, an attempt was actually made to 'bend' the tower back, so to speak, by building vertically again. Surprising as it may seem the tower is actually in no danger of collapsing (it is continuously monitored and receives injections of concrete when necessary). In the words of an Italian song, *'Evviva la Torre di Pisa, che pende, che pende e mai non vien giù'* (Hurrah! for the Tower of Pisa, it leans and it leans but it doesn't fall down).

The baptistry: Despite its size the baptistry, facing the cathedral, avoids any impression of heaviness; it is a fine, elegant building decorated with figures, columns and arches. It was originally designed, according to an inscription, by the architect Diotisalvi, and the first of the eight columns brought from Elba and Sardinia was raised in 1163. Following a break in construction Nicola Pisano took charge in 1260, introducing a Gothic influence. But it was not until the end of the 14th c. that the dome (55 m) was completed. The *bottega* of Nicola and Giovanni Pisano and their assistants was responsible for the wealth of figurative ornamentation. In the interior (font and altar) the *pulpit* to which Nicola Pisano put his signature in 1260 effectively initiated Gothic sculpture in

Tuscany. For amongst his assistants were his son Giovanni and Arnolfo di Cambio, both soon to make their own contributions to the emergence of Gothic art in the building of Florence Cathedral.

Camposanto: At the north side of the great square lies the perfectly rectangular Camposanto, its inner court still the cemetery created in 1203 by Archbishop Ubaldo with earth brought by ship from Mount Golgotha. The cloisters (begun in 1277) were badly damaged by American artillery fire in the last war and the famous frescos have been in process of restoration for many years. They include the *Trionfo della Morte* (Triumph of Death) at one time attributed to the painter Orcagna but now believed to be by Francesco Traini. Benozzo Gozzoli was responsible (1468–84) for twenty-three narrative frescos (the *Tower of Babel* being the most notable), but the huge Camposanto wall-paintings

Camposanto

are really more a gallery of work by dozens of Tuscan and Umbrian masters from the 14th to the 16th c. In addition the cemetery is like an open-air museum of marble sculptures and grave statuary dating back over many centuries.

Citadel: The view over Pisa from the citadel, with the hills of Monte S. Giuliano and Monte Pisano in the background, reveals the broad (and not entirely pristine) Arno

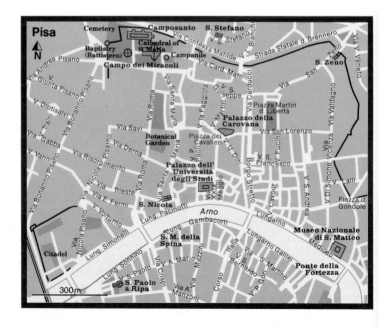

winding its way through the city under the Ponte Solferino. On the riverbank are the outlines of *S. Maria della Spina*, begun in 1323 as an oratory to house a *spina* (thorn) from Christ's crown of thorns. A hundred years ago the small, elaborate marble building, an exquisite cameo of Gothic craftsmanship, was almost destroyed by flood waters from the Arno and had to be rebuilt piece by piece. This part of Pisa, on the far side of the Arno from the Leaning Tower, harbours further delights: a dozen churches (of which *S. Nicola, S. Paolo a Ripa* and *S. Zeno* most reward a visit).

The town centre lies between the *Piazza dei Cavalieri* — with the *Palazzo della Carovana* and church of *S. Stefano* — and the arrestingly scenic Arno embankment *(Lungarno)* with its imposing house fronts and its bridges. Many of Pisa's original 13th

Pisa from the Leaning Tower

Top: Archbishop's palace
Above: Palazzo dei Cavalieri

and 14th c. frescos and sculptures are now in the *Museo Nazionale di S. Matteo* in the old Benedictine monastery (on the embankment beside the *Ponte della Fortezza*). The *Palazzo dei Cavalieri* (also called the *Palazzo della Carovana*), rebuilt in princely style by Giorgio Vasari (1562), is still the home of the *Scuola normale superiore*, Italy's élite college founded by Napoleon. The *University* of Pisa, established in 1329, always enjoyed the patronage of the Medici and later became a powerhouse of liberal ideas. It remains one of Italy's major centres for research, the main building being in the *Palazzo dell'Università degli Studi* (Via XXIX Maggio). Numerous institutes and science museums are affiliated to it, including the *Botanical Garden* (Via Luca Ghini).

Gioco del Ponte; Regata storica di S. Ranieri (1st Sunday in June).

Sergio, 1 Lungarno Pacinotti (tel. 050/48 245).

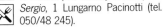

From Tuscany to Umbria

From Florence — Tuscany's chief town — to Perugia — provincial capital of Umbria — the road goes via Arezzo, following not only a geographical logic but a kind of cultural logic as well. Despite the present regional boundaries these three glorious medieval cities belong together as a triumvirate. In earlier times their art and their artists, from Giotto to Raphael, were engaged in lively exchange. Florence of course eventually outshone the others — as it still does today.

Leave Florence by the Autostrada del Sole, following it through lovely scenery in which plains alternate with gentle slopes along the valley of the Arno, here and there passing close to enchanting Tuscan manor houses. In the last fifteen years a vigorous industrialisation has taken place along both sides of the motorway, stimulated by the great 'artery' as it is called and injecting new blood into the regional economy. Even so this big road is far from overcrowded. To the left is the chain of mountains called Pratomagno, part of the central Apennines; to the right are the hills of the Chianti district. Ahead, the Arno valley and the Chiana valley meet.

Arezzo Pop. 92,000

Arezzo, once a rival to Florence, now an industrial city, is spread over the slopes of hills some 300 m above the confluence of the upper Arno and Chiana valleys in the plain below. Patience is needed when coming from the Autostrada del Sole: one still has to face 10 km of heavy traffic before reaching the lower city gate, the best place to leave the car.

 A walk round the town

Arezzo has three great attractions, one of which is a real gem.

S. Francesco (Piazza S. Francesco) is a basilica church whose great glory is the renowned series of frescos by Piero della Francesca. Behind a very plain façade the interior reveals itself as a fine Gothic hall, its walls richly decorated. Go straight to the *choir chapels* while you are still alert and fresh: Piero della Francesca's *Legend of the Holy Cross* is one of the most important works of the entire Italian Renaissance. The fresco cycle, based on the medieval legend of the recovery of the True Cross, was painted in the years between 1453 and 1464 at a time when the city was experiencing a period of great prosperity. It weaves a narrative thread between Adam's death and the Queen of Sheba, between Solomon and Constantine, between Arezzo and Jerusalem, following the account given in the *Legenda Aurea*. In the hands of Piero della Francesca the human figure attains new heights of expressiveness, far exceeding those of mere allegory. Painstaking restoration work has achieved wonders here. The significance of this great artist was only recognised at the turn of the century, and the frescos were in danger of being lost.

Now make your way through the town's steep streets to the delightful *Piazza Grande* (filled with antique-shops) and so to the next port of call.

Cathedral of S. Donato: more frescos by Piero della Francesca. On leaving be sure

Arezzo

to include a visit to the *fortezza* from which there is a most beautiful view over the town.

On the way back to the car there are a number of other fine buildings to be seen and at least one further visit to be made.

Painting by Piero della Francesca in S. Francesco

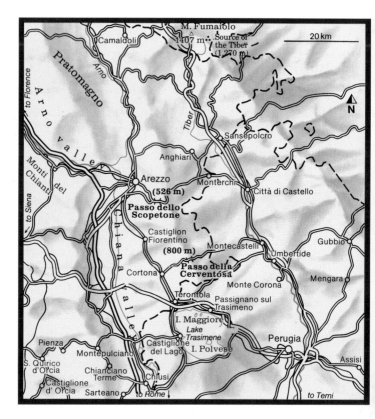

Palazzo Pretorio: nowadays the town library with a collection of manuscripts. The façade is profusely ornamented with coats of arms.

The poet Francesco Petrarch was born in Arezzo; so too were the satirist Pietro Aretino and, very much earlier, the refined Etruscan Maecenas, generous patron of literature and the arts. There is a saying *'Aretini, cervelli fini'*: 'the people of Arezzo are of noble intellect'.

 Giostra del Saracino (September).

 Il Cantuccio, 76 Via Madonna del Prato (tel. 0 575/26 830); *Continen-* *tale*, 7 Piazza Guido Monaco (tel. 0 575/20 251); *Minerva*, 2/6 Via Fiorentina (tel. 0 575/27 891).

Ex Excursions

To appreciate fully the loveliness and variety of rural Tuscany and Umbria you must pluck up the courage to leave the main intercity highways and take to the country roads. Your reward will be finding a world from which modern progress has not yet dispelled the romance. Here are two suggestions for motorists who enjoy the simple things, and for whom the journey from one place to another is as important as the arrival.

A special tip

Camaldoli, set in the middle of dense forests over 800 m above sea-level (50 km from Arezzo), is the famous monastery where in 1012 St Romualdo founded the Camaldolese order. It was to meetings here that Lorenzo the Magnificent and Leon Battista Alberti later summoned the great minds of their humanist Academy. The monks' cells are situated higher up, away from the *foresteria* where strangers are welcomed. You can visit the superb buildings and buy herb schnapps from the distillery.

Città di Castello (42 km): Leave Arezzo heading east along the SS 73 (Senese Aretina), skirting slopes covered with olive-groves and vineyards and then crossing the low pass at Foce di Scopetone (526 m). Continue in the direction of Monterchi, turning off onto the SS 221 which leads through Monterchi to Città di Castello (see page 65).

Sansepolcro (38 km): Take the pretty and not too twisting SS 73 which crosses the Passo dello Scopetone. Further along, over to the right, can be seen Monterchi, a very old hill village with a castle, and shortly afterwards the town of Anghiari comes into view. Not far beyond, on the other side of the Tiber, lies the small town of Sansepolcro (see page 65).

After visiting Arezzo a good route to follow is the SS 71 which bypasses Castiglion Fiorentino on its way to Cortona, a hill town some 30 km away.

Palazzo Pretorio, Arezzo

Anghiari

Cortona

Cortona Pop. 23,000

Cortona is situated on a rocky spur (500 m) overlooking the Chiana valley. It is still enclosed in places by the Etruscan walls on which the present bastions were later erected. These afford magnificent views.

 What to see

The buildings of the Old Town cluster round the central *Piazza della Repubblica*. The

Cortona Museum – Fra Angelico, Adoration of the Magi

Palazzo Comunale was already in existence there in 1241 though it has been repeatedly altered since. On one side its arcades look out onto the Piazza Signorelli in which the *Etruscan Museum* can be found, housed in the *Palazzo Pretorio*. Quite exceptional among its exhibits is the huge bronze lamp dating from the 6th c. BC which was discovered by farm workers during the last century. A little further down is the *cathedral* with its plain façade, perhaps designed by Sangallo. Opposite the cathedral the *Diocesan Museum* has among its possessions an altarpiece by Fra Angelico. The Cortona-born painter Luca Signorelli was his pupil. The museum contains the diocesan art collection.

The streets and alleyways between Cortona's sandstone houses are so steep that the town's only level thoroughfare bears a name announcing the fact! The *Passeggiata in piano*, which runs from behind the church of S. Domenico for a good kilometre or more, offers some lovely views. A sweeping panorama can also be obtained from the *Medici fortress*, high above the Old Town, from where the sight of Lake Trasimene in the distance brings to mind thoughts of Hannibal. Outside the town is the fine Renaissance church of the Madonna del Calcinaio.

 La Loggetta, Piazza Peschiera (tel. 0 575/603 777).

From Cortona rejoin the SS 71 and head for Terontola on Lake Trasimene.

Lake Trasimene

Lake Trasimene *(Lago Trasimeno)* promises a pleasant day, not just in summer but at any time of year, and anyone driving northwards from Chiusi into the Chiana valley will find the detour well worth while. The lake, the biggest in central Italy (128 sq km), lies at the foot of gently rolling hills. Castiglione del Lago is the largest of the lakeside resorts, though Passignano sul Trasimeno is an attractive place too. The lake is uniformly shallow, only 6 m at its deepest point, but it abounds with fish and several of its villages have inviting fish restaurants. It is actually a delightful vestige of a vast area of swamp which the Etruscans and Romans repeatedly tried to drain to create fertile arable land. The Romans were eventually successful, drawing the water off south-eastwards through an extensive subterranean drainage channel.

There are three islands in the lake, the

Lake Trasimene

northernmost being Isola Maggiore (the largest, as the name suggests). A few hundred people, fishermen, craftsmen and their families, live on it in a picturesque village where there are a number of things worth seeing. The women of the island make beautiful lace. Of the other two islands Isola Minore has fewer attractions than Isola Polvese in the south-east corner. This has recently been acquired by the Perugia council and opened to the public as a park. There is a medieval castle and some ruined churches, and the whole place is a tranquil haven of burgeoning greenery. In Castiglione del Lago and Passignano sul Trasimeno there are rowing- and motorboats for hire; or you can take a trip on the steamer which operates throughout the summer and late into autumn.

Madonna del Calcinaio, Cortona

 A piece of history

So what about Hannibal? The swampland (in the midst of which a river created the huge lake, the fourth largest in Italy) was the scene of the Romans' greatest defeat. Hannibal and his army had spent the winter of 217 BC at Fiesole. In the spring he suddenly appeared, marching down the Arno valley heading for Rome, bypassing the camp of the Roman consul Flaminius. Hannibal had ordered his light cavalry to take up position in the hills around Cortona, and from there in the early morning mist they fell upon the pursuing Roman troops. 16,000 Roman legionaries perished in the battle against the Carthaginians.

Today the lake is a popular summer resort, the epitome of peacefulness, far removed from the strife of war. It seems much more in keeping that St Francis of Assisi once fasted on one of the islands in the lake. He returned on Good Friday after forty-two days and, lo and behold, of the two loaves he had taken with him he had eaten only half of one of them. To this day a festival is still held to celebrate the marvel.

 Sauro, Isola Maggiore (tel. 075/826 168).

At Lake Trasimene the SS 71 meets the SS 75 bis which goes on to Perugia.

Perugia Pop. 144,000

Perugia is the provincial capital of Umbria, an administrative centre and a university city; in short, it is the focal point of the region—a fact of which it is proudly aware. The Old Town on its steep, irregularly shaped hill is splendidly preserved, still very much lived in and bustling with activity.

For more than 2,000 years, throughout its chequered history of Etruscans and Romans, of Byzantines, Lombards and feudal lords, and of the 14th c. independent community with its powerful guilds, Perugia has always been the region's dominant town.

Detail of the Fontana Maggiore

 The town centre

Cathedral square: Climbing the steep approach to the cathedral square we immediately see evidence of Perugia's heyday in the 14th c. In front of the Gothic *Cattedrale di San Lorenzo* — the exterior though unfinished is actually more impressive than the inside — stands the beautiful *Fontana Maggiore*, a 13th c. masterpiece by Nicola and Giovanni Pisano. In the programme of bas-reliefs decorating the exterior of the basin two seated female figures personify the federated cities of Rome and Perugia.

The large square is surrounded by magnificent palazzi, the most celebrated being the *Palazzo dei Priori* (or *Palazzo Comunale*) which houses Umbria's principal art gallery, the *Galleria Nazionale dell'Umbria*. Over two dozen superb rooms form such a vast treasure-house of paintings by artists of the Umbrian and Tuscan schools that there is only space to mention the most important names: Duccio di Buoninsegna, Meo di Guido da Siena, Giotto, Lippo Vanni, Taddeo

Palazzo dei Priori

di Bartolo, Gentile da Fabriano, Beato Angelico, Piero della Francesca, Benozzo Gozzoli, Francesco di Giorgio Martini and the greatest of all Perugian painters, Pietro Vannucci, known as *il Perugino*. (A pupil of Verrocchio's in Florence, he was in turn Raphael's teacher.) Incorporated into the museum is the *Antica Cappella dei Priori*, its frescos by Benedetto Bonfigli showing how Perugia itself looked during the Renaissance. The Palazzo dei Priori is also the home of Perugia's council and is truly magnificent. Don't miss the *Sala dei Notari* on the first floor, where the townspeople and later the notaries of the city held their assemblies.

Corso Vannucci: After visiting the gallery (don't stint on time!) return to the cathedral square for a leisurely walk down the wide Corso Vannucci (as the students and Perugians themselves do whenever they

Students on the cathedral steps

particular there is an incomparable view over the wide valley towards Assisi and the Sibilline mountains.

The lower city

For those with time at their disposal there are numerous other things to see: the church of *S. Giuliana* (Via XX Settembre), the *Porta Marzia* and the Renaissance fortress of *Rocca Paolina* (Via Marzia), which Pope Paul III Farnese erected over the palaces of the feudal Baglioni family (remains of these buildings can be seen in the subterranean *Via Baglioni*), the *Museo Archeologico Nazionale dell'Umbria* (Piazza Giordano Bruno), and the *Basilica di S. Pietro* and *Porta S. Pietro* (Borgo XX Giugno).

On any of these walks it is impossible not to notice how full the city is of young people from all over the world: 20,000 students attend Perugia's old *university*, founded in the 14th c., which today has fourteen faculties; and in addition, 8,000 language students are attracted to the University for Foreigners. This makes life in the city extremely lively and at times somewhat chaotic.

(The Registry of the University for Foreigners is in the Palazzo Gallenga, Piazza Fortebraccio, 06100 Perugia).

have an hour to spare). Almost immediately you come upon the entrance to the *Sala del Collegio della Mercanzia*, which the city put at the disposal of the guild of merchants in 1390. A little further along the Corso is the *Palazzo del Collegio dei Notari* and, opposite, the *Collegio del Cambio*, meeting house of the bankers' guild. The entrance leads into the *Sala dell'Udienza del Cambio*, the former exchange. Dark wooden benches with intarsia inlays make an elegant contrast to the colourful frescos, Perugino's finest masterpieces. The archives — still intact — include the artist's receipt for payment in the year 1507: 350 gold ducats. The figure of Daniel (on the right-hand wall) is believed to be a portrait of Raphael, assumed to have been one of Perugino's assistants on the project.

After enjoying this great feast of art continue between the beautiful *palazzi* to the far end of the Corso Vannucci and then out onto the terrace of the small gardens beyond. The local people regard this spot as the real heart of Umbria. At sundown in

 Paradis d'été.

 Open-air theatre; Umbrian music festival (September).

 Children's amusement park (Città della Domenica — open the whole year).

 Falchetto, 20 Via Bartolo (tel. 075/61 875); *La Lanterna*, 6 Via Rocchi (tel. 075/66 064); *Ricciotto*, Piazza Danti (tel. 075/21 965); *La Taverna*, 8 Via delle Streghe (tel. 075/61 028).

From the hilltop town of Urbino

The upper Tiber valley

The drive north from Perugia is a chance to explore the Tiber valley, one of the most picturesque areas of Italy. It has the advantage of being neither overrun by tourists nor heavily populated. Since Roman times one of the consular roads, the Tiberina, has followed this stretch of the river which Horace called the *flavus Tiberis*, the 'blond Tiber'.

By the time it nears Perugia the famous river has 90 km of its 400-km course behind it and is already powerful. The Tiberina, following the river upstream through gently undulating country, is a wide road offering comfortable driving. On the left rises the oak-covered Monte Corona; to the right tobacco plantations are interspersed with olive-groves and cornfields.

Numerous castles and also some monasteries are hidden away in the hills around the little town of Umbertide, some in ruins, some converted into private villas. Among the many detours which could be made here, the one to Gubbio should definitely not be missed. Beyond Umbertide the Tiber valley recasts its spell, alternately narrowing and then widening, leading first to Città di Castello and from there to Sansepolcro.

Anyone intent on paying full honours to the Tiber should make the excursion from Sansepolcro to Monte Fumaiolo where the river has its source (at a height of 1,270 m). There are two gushing springs which quickly join forces to begin their journey to the plain.

From the top of Monte Fumaiolo (1,409 m) there is an unrivalled view to be enjoyed, looking south down the Tiber valley and eastwards to San Marino and Urbino — up here is the roof of central Italy.

From Perugia the SS 3 bis (Tiberina) heads north to where the SS 219 turns off, a few kilometres before Umbertide. The road runs alongside the little River Assino, in a narrow valley flanked by forested hills, eventually climbing to a height of almost 1,000 m. To left and right are numerous castles, tiny ramshackle villages and clusters of houses. Ahead at the end of this nowadays seldom used route is a medieval town without parallel, Gubbio.

Gubbio Pop. 32,300

Gubbio is separated from Perugia by some of the most delightful countryside imaginable, the scenic highpoint of which is the town itself, clinging to the wooded hillside of Monte Ingino. Having managed for centuries to preserve its character and its great wealth of art treasures and architecture, Gubbio is now reaping its reward in the shape of a continuously growing stream of admirers. Everyone goes about on foot, and for a good reason — the streets climb so steeply! Everywhere you look there is so much to see that a one-day visit is scarcely enough.

 What to see

Even before reaching the junction of the Via Matteotti, *Madonna del Prato* is in view — the first of almost two dozen churches. To the left the Via Mausoleo leads to the grim memorial dedicated to the *Quaranta Martiri*, victims of an act of reprisal by the Germans during the last war.

Whichever way you now choose to proceed, either keeping to the steep streets or taking a roundabout route via alleyways and stone steps, the point to be aimed for is the *Piazza della Signoria*. The towering *Palazzo dei Consoli* signals your arrival, with the *Palazzo Pretorio* on its left and, to the right, the *Palazzo Ranghiasci-Brancaleone*. The entire long side of the piazza forms a splendid terrace from which to look out over the tiled roofs of the city to the remains of the Roman amphitheatre

and the broad plain beyond.

The *Palazzo dei Consoli*, one of the finest civic palaces in Italy, was designed (as one can read on the main door) between 1332 and 1337, probably by Angelo da Orvieto. Wide steps lead up to the huge *Salone*, which occupies the whole extent of the Palazzo, and is where the citizens used to meet. Among the exhibits in the *Museo Civico* (town museum) housed in the building are the renowned *Eugubine Marbles*, seven bronze tablets inscribed with details of religious ceremonies, partly in Etruscan-Umbrian and partly in Latin characters. To scholars of ancient history they remain one of the most puzzling testaments from the past. A precarious-looking staircase seemingly suspended in the air goes up to the *Pinacoteca Comunale*, a gallery of 15th and 16th c. paintings.

The *Palazzo Pretorio* (opposite, built in 1349, also known as the Palazzo dei Priori, is now the council offices. From there the Gothic *Palazzo del Bargello* (in medieval times the equivalent of a police station) is reached by descending the broad, curving Via dei Consoli. Passing the many austere but beautiful palaces en route, keep a look-out for one of the famous *Porte del Morto*, small doors with pointed arches and no steps which used only to be opened to allow a corpse to be brought out and were then immediately locked again.

From the Via dei Consoli it is only a short distance to the *cathedral*, likewise Gothic, and the *Palazzo Ducale* opposite, the origins of which date back to Lombard

Gubbio

times. It was altered and enlarged in 1476 by Federico da Montefeltro, who apparently modelled it on his ducal palace in nearby Urbino. Inside the recently and excellently restored building is a superb inner courtyard with an unusual interplay of colour between its *pietra serena* (light stonework) and red brick.

 Town of festivals

A one-hour walk (or a six-minute ride by cable-car from Porta Romana) brings you to the *Basilica di S. Ubaldo* (830 m up), dedicated to the town's patron saint (Franciscan monastery, fine doorway and cloister). Here the famous *ceri* are kept until brought out for use in Gubbio's extraordinary religious festival, the *Corso dei Ceri*. Originally the ceri were simply bundles of candles carried up to the church in honour of the saint by members of the three guilds. Since then however they have become

huge, complicated wooden constructions, 6 to 7 m tall, on top of which are mounted effigies of the patron saints of the guilds. On the first Sunday in May these exceptionally heavy contraptions are brought into the town in preparation for the race, the *Corsa dei Ceri*, held on May 15th. After seemingly interminable preliminaries, on the stroke of twelve and to an accompaniment of wildly ringing bells, the giant pillars are hoisted onto the shoulders of the *ceraioli*, who are dressed in multi-coloured costumes, and carried through the streets. At 6 pm the *ceri* are shouldered again, this time to be consecrated at the entrance to the cathedral before the *ceraioli* race through the alleyways to the Piazza della Signoria. After a rest, a signal from the mayor starts them off once more, racing at a gallop up the steep slopes of Monte Ingino back to St Ubaldo's Basilica. The fastest take a mere thirteen minutes for the ascent, which in normal circumstances takes an

Interior of the Palazzo dei Consoli, Gubbio

hour! A second traditional festival takes place on the last Sunday in May — the *Palio della Balestra*, a crossbow tournament in medieval costume held on the Piazza della Signoria.

However, culture in Gubbio does not only live in the past. In July and August there is open-air opera in the Roman amphitheatre, and October sees the presentation of an international prize for literature. The second Sunday in every month is devoted to a small antiques fair, and the town also has a biennial ceramics and metalwork exhibition (in August and September). There is no shortage of excuses for hurrying off to Gubbio!

Dei Consoli, 59 Via dei Consoli (tel. 075/9 273 335); *Funivia*, Via Monte Ingino (tel. 075/9 273 464); *Porta Tessenaca*, 21 Via Picardi (tel. 075/9 272 765); *Taverna del Lupo*, 21 Via Ansidei (tel. 075/9 274 368).

From Gubbio drive back to Umbertide, the small town situated in the middle of the prettiest part of the upper Tiber valley, only 30 km from Perugia.

Umbertide Pop. 13,500

Dominated by the ruins of a fortress (1385) Umbertide remains in essence a medieval town. It also has one or two pleasing surprises for art-lovers. Inside the church of *S. Croce* is Signorelli's great *Deposition from the Cross*, and in *S. Francesco* there is a *Madonna and Saints* by Pomarancio (1577). Within easy reach of the town are the castle of *Civitella Ranieri* (5 km northeast) and in Monte Corona (6 km south) the thousand-year-old abbey of *S. Salvatore*, founded by St Romualdo in the year 1008 (early 15th c. frescos).

 Excursion to Cortona (47 km)
Take the SS 3 bis over the 800-m-high Passo della Cerventosa and from there to the hill town of Cortona (see page 56). Although the road is very winding, the scenery is superb.

From Umbertide continue to Città di Castello, keeping to the Tiberina which is pleasanter than the dual carriageway.

Città di Castello Pop. 37,900
The unmistakable outline of Città di Castello's compact town centre can be seen from afar. It is one of only a few towns situated in the plain.

 What to see
The fortress tower, campanile and octagonal cathedral dome soar into the sky from within an almost complete 15th to 17th c. town wall. The massive arch of the *Porta S. Maria Maggiore* leads through into the main promenade, the Corso Vittorio Emanuele. At its end is the upper square, the *Piazza di Sopra*, surrounded by Renaissance palaces and the Gothic *Palazzo del Podestà* whose well-preserved façade (the work of Angelo da Orvieto) looks directly onto the Corso Cavour. This Corso in turn opens on to the *Piazza di Sotto*, the lower square, with its impressive Gothic *Palazzo Comunale* (1334–52), also by Angelo da Orvieto. Joined to the Palazzo is the ancient cathedral of *SS. Florido e Amanzio* dedicated to Città di Castello's patron saints. A variety of stylistic elements have been added to the building over the years. From the cathedral doorway turn left along the Via dei Casceri and then left again to the *Palazzo Vitelli alla Cannoniera* (built by Antonio da Sangallo), one of five palaces which belonged to the ruling Vitelli family.

The *Cannoniera*, its superb 16th c. exterior and interior both beautifully preserved, houses the municipal *Pinacoteca* which has some fine furniture and valuable paintings. Among the most interesting are an early Raphael — a painted standard depicting the *Creation of Eve* (1501) — and *St Sebastian* by Luca Signorelli.

After enjoying the art collection take a walk along the town's fortification walls to admire the largest of the Vitelli palaces, the *Palazzo Vitelli a S. Egidio*, built by Giorgio Vasari in 1540. A whole complex of gardens is enclosed within including a graceful little pavilion, the *Palazzina*.

 International festival of chamber music (end of August to September).

 Tiferno, 13 Piazza Raffaello Sanzio (tel. 075/8 550 331/8 550 349).

Another effortless drive on the Tiberina brings you to Sansepolcro, and thus back into Tuscany.

Sansepolcro Pop, 15,600
Sansepolcro has been famous since the 15th c. as the birthplace of Piero della Francesca. On the Piazza Torre di Berta there is a medieval tower — the *Berta* — which stands all alone like a jilted bride. Sansepolcro also has a fine *cathedral* and several well-preserved old palazzi, including the *Palazzo delle Laudi*. The municipal art collection in the *Pinacoteca* includes some important works by Piero della Francesca, in particular the *Resurrection*. Above the town stands a Medici fortress.

 Palio della Balestra (crossbow tournament) in September.

From Sansepolcro there is a pleasant drive to Arezzo by way of Anghiari along the pretty and not too twisting SS 73. The road goes over a little pass, the Passo dello Scopetone (just over 500 m), before which Monterchi, a very old village with a castle, can be seen on a hill to the left.

Assisi

South of Perugia

Even today the region to the south of Perugia gives the impression of having been left to its own devices for a lengthy period; it is a place apart, away from the world of trade and commerce, for all that the Tiber's great waterway traverses its entire length. An air of rural charm and tranquillity reigns in the smaller towns — Spello, Bevagna and Montefalco up on their heights, and the places in the south on the slopes of the Monti Martani. The larger towns such as Foligno and Spoleto have begun to feel the breath of change and are now making more of tourism, but in the side valleys many places still remain almost undisturbed.

Along its middle section the Tiber has fashioned a fertile plain known as the Valle Umbra through which the new Superstrada E 7 now runs. It follows the line of the old Tiberina, making it quite easy to visit the most interesting towns — Assisi, Todi, Terni, Orvieto — in quick succession. It is precisely here however that some worthwhile detours can be made, into the Nera valley for example, the remote south-east corner of Umbria; to Norcia, birthplace of St Benedict; or over the hills from Todi across south Umbria to Orvieto (46 km on the SS 79 bis, Orvietana).

The direct route follows the fast road from Perugia to nearby Assisi (27 km).

Assisi Alt. 424 m; pop. 24,700

Assisi clings to the slopes of a spur of Monte Subasio, every bit a picture-post-card scene. The high walls of the *Basilica di S. Francesco* with their fortress-like ram- parts, gates and towers are visible from a considerable distance away. It is not known who designed the basilica, but in 1253 while still unfinished it was dedicated to St Francis of Assisi (see page 69).

What to see

Basilica di S. Francesco: The *Lower Church* was partly hewn out of the rock, and the *Upper Church* (with a lovely façade) and the *campanile* were built just above it. The whole complex of buildings represents a veritable hoard of art treasures, and detailed tours are conducted by the monks (daily, 9 am–12 noon and 2–6 pm). In the *Lower Church* the third chapel on the right (frescos by Giotto), the vaulting above the main altar (also decorated by Giotto and his school) and the frescos in the south transept are all exceptional. The first chapel on the left has celebrated wall-paintings (1322–26) by Simone Martini, radiating a gentle charm.

The superb fresco cycle in the north transept, apse and south transept of the *Upper Church* was begun by Cimabue in about 1277. Tragically some of it is in very poor condition, the colours having deteriorated with time.

Basilica di S. Francesco

In the nave is Giotto's *Life of St Francis*, a cycle of twenty-eight frescos, most of which were painted by the master himself with some by his pupils (see page 70).

A walk round the town

A walk round Assisi takes you by way of the Via S. Francesco to the other end of the elongated town (15 minutes), to the *cathedral* (Piazza S. Rufino) —

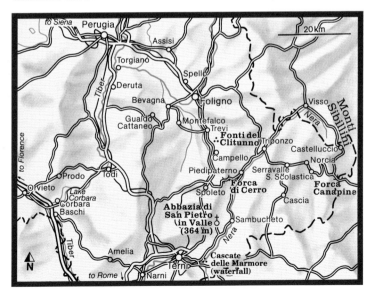

Assisi

impressive with its austere façade — and the *Museo Capitolare* nearby.

Santa Chiara: The *Basilica di Santa Chiara*, a short distance away from the cathedral, is the feminine equivalent, so to speak, of that of S. Francesco; it is a building of Gothic elegance (completed in 1265) with some elaborately decorated chapels and the relics of St Clare to whom it is dedicated. There is a splendid panoramic view of the town and the plain of Topino.

On the way back go past the *Vescovado* (bishop's palace) and along the Via Borgo S. Pietro past the *Convento di S. Giuseppe* to the Romanesque-Gothic Benedictine church of *S. Pietro*.

Eremo delle Carceri: Around Assisi there are numerous other sites rich in religious associations of one sort or another. One of these, the *Eremo delle Carceri*, is only 4 km from the *Porta dei Cappuccini*. The walk there promises enchantment by both art and nature!

Anyone with enough time should also visit the church of *S. Maria degli Angeli*, in which St Francis preached, and the *Rocca Maggiore*, the fortress high above the town. The Roman *amphitheatre* and the *Temple of Minerva* are reminders of Assisi's even more ancient past.

It will take a stay of three to four days to do justice to Assisi and the many places of interest nearby.

Religious festivals

No matter what the time of year there will almost certainly be some form of religious celebration taking place here. On the night of April 30th/May 1st there is a procession through the narrow streets with much music and song, recalling, as tradition has it, St Francis' own homage to 'the Madonna Poverty'. At Corpus Christi the streets are strewn with flowers, while between July 31st and August 2nd people from all around gather to take part in devotional night vigils. On the first Sunday in September there is a medieval pageant celebrating St Francis' return to his birthplace, and on October 3rd and 4th Italians from all over the country honour the patron saint of all Italy by bringing oil for the eternal flame above his grave.

 Fontemaggio.

Buca di S. Francesco, 1 Via Brizi (tel. 075/812 204); *La Fontana da Carletto*, 8 Via S. Francesco (tel. 075/812 933); *Il Medievo*, Piazza del Comune (tel. 075/813 068); *Taverna dell'Arco da Bino*, 8 Via S. Gregorio (tel. 075/812 383); *Umbra*, 6 Vicolo degli Archi (tel. 075/812 240); *Del Viaggiatore*, 2 Via S. Antonio (tel. 075/812 424).

Leaving Assisi go back to rejoin the E 7. A fast drive bypassing Torgiano and Deruta soon brings you to the turn-off for Todi.

St Francis of Assisi and Giotto

'Come, Francis, repair my Church! Do you not see that it collapses?' These words, heard while he was in deep contemplation of the cross in the little church of S. Damiano, started St Francis of Assisi on his mission to bring spiritual regeneration to the Church.

He was born in Assisi in 1182, the son of a rich cloth merchant, and after a happy and somewhat dissipated youth fought as a knight in the skirmishes between Assisi and Perugia. Imprisonment and a serious illness prompted his conversion to piety. Having received Christ's summons in the first of many mystical visions, Francis hurried home, took some of his father's bales of cloth, sold them in the neighbouring town of Foligno and gave the proceeds for the rebuilding of S. Damiano. His wealthy father saw only wastefulness in such action and reported his son to the bishop. Francis responded by removing all his own clothes and returning them to his father. From then on he was to be satisfied with a brown habit tied with a cord, the same clothing, in fact, that was worn by the poor peasants of Umbria. So came into being the monkish garb of the Franciscans, the order he founded as more and more followers came to join him. Francis preached poverty, chastity and obedience, his call to poverty bestowing a higher significance and worth upon the condition which most people in the Middle Ages were forced to endure. These ideas did not easily gain acceptance, however. Missionary journeys took the saint and his twelve disciples all over Italy as well as to Egypt, Syria and Spain. Eventually the rules of the Minorite (Franciscan) order were approved by Pope Honorius III who also recognised the sister order of the Poor Clares, which was established by Francis' 'spiritual sister' St Clare. Towards the end of his life, after many illnesses and deprivations which he accepted cheerfully, Francis received the stigmata. He was canonised in 1228, only two years after his death.

To St Francis is also owed the glorious *Canticle of the Creatures* (*Cantico delle creature*), the first Italian vernacular poem, in fact a rhythmic prose song — it is presumed to have been set to music — filled with adoration for all God's creatures. The canticle soon became the 'signature tune' of the Franciscans who travelled the country preaching the joy of God's creation. In stark contrast to the ascetic literature of the period which saw only evil in worldly things, the canticle hymns the praises of the elements and the stars, of the wind and of death. They are the brothers and sisters of mankind. It was composed by Francis after a night of dreadful suffering, as we know from a later Latin biography, and from a late 14th c. anthology, *The Little Flowers of St Francis*, written in the Tuscan dialect. The painter Giotto recorded the legend of St Francis too, in his marvellous cycle of frescos in the church of *S. Francesco* in Assisi.

The historian Gregorovius wrote later: 'The masterly hand of Giotto represented the saint's espousal of poverty, in a charming painting above his grave in Assisi; yet the great founder of this begging order was already lying in a glittering gold and marble church. His mendicant friars were soon living in richly endowed monasteries everywhere; poverty remained on the other side of the monastery gates...'

The Church had in fact decided to regard St Francis not as a heretic but as a useful teacher, a man who breathed new life into religion and enriched the supply of topics for sermons — indeed the Brothers were soon sought after as preachers. But the true spirit of St Francis is brought to us in the lines of the *Canticle of the Creatures*:

Lord be praised,
By all Your creation,
First by noble Brother Sun,
Who brings us the day and gives us
Light with his glorious rays;
So splendid is his powerful radiance
That he is as Your image, O Father on high.

Lord be praised,
By Brother Wind
And air and clouds and rain,
Who, mild or severe, according to Your will,
Govern all the beings of Your creation.

Lord be praised,
By our sister, Mother Earth,
Who supports us steadfastly and well,
And offers us every kind of fruit
With colourful flowers and meadows.

St Francis of Assisi: part of the *Canticle of the Creatures*

Giotto di Bondone (1266–1337) was not the first artist commissioned to decorate the church at Assisi; the great Cimabue for example had already contributed his majestic wall-paintings (only a few of which have survived) both to the Lower Church where the saint's body was entombed and later to the Upper Church as well. It is possible that Giotto worked on them while he was apprenticed to Cimabue. But if today we are able to picture the saint vividly to ourselves it is Giotto we have to thank. Exactly how many of the paintings in the cycle on the life of St Francis were personally executed by Giotto, and how many were painted by assistants working to his designs, is a matter of some dispute. What the frescos demonstrate beyond question, however, is that the aura and powerful legend surrounding the saint inspired the artist to free himself from the rigidly stylised art of his day, and to make use of vivid, natural settings to 'tell' of events in St Francis' life. A simple man honouring the young Francis on the Piazza Grande — the saint handing his fine clothes to his father in the presence of the bishop — Pope Innocent III dreaming of how St Francis holds up the collapsing Lateran Palace — the saint appearing to his disciples in a chariot of fire — the saint driving the devils out of Arezzo — St Francis preaching to the birds — the Poor Clares mourning the death of the saint; these are just some of the themes which make up the cycle.

Todi Pop. 17,400

What is now the *Piazza Vittorio Emanuele II* has been the heart of the city ever since Roman times — under the present paving-stones are the remains of what was once the forum. In the Middle Ages Todi made itself impregnable, four gates providing the only access to the world outside its walls.

 ### What to see

Much the best viewpoint from which to take in the cluster of old buildings in the town centre is from the east corner of the Piazza: on the right stands the *Palazzo dei Priori*, opposite are the *Palazzo del Popolo* and the *Palazzo del Capitano*, and to the left a tall flight of wide steps leads up to the *cathedral*.

The *Palazzo del Popolo* is a fine building of Gothic purity, begun in 1213 but with a bell-tower added some time later. The *Palazzo del Capitano*, started about 1290, houses the municipal art gallery and the *Etruscan and Roman Museum*. Its external staircase also gives access to the former assembly hall in the adjoining *Palazzo del Popolo*. Be sure also to search out the *Piazza della Repubblica* from where stone steps lead to gardens and the church of *S. Fortunato*. A chapel inside the church is decorated with a fresco by Masolino da Panicale, *Madonna and Child with Angels*.

As you leave the town there is one final architectural delight in store, the Renaissance church of *S. Maria della Consolazione* which towers majestically outside the town gates. It is a wonderfully elegant central-plan building attributed to Bramante.

Todi however is best known not so much for its buildings as for being the birthplace of the 13th c. Franciscan monk Jacopone da Todi, composer of the profoundly religious *Laudi* and the *Stabat Mater (Il pianto della Madonna)* traditionally sung during Easter week.

 Antiques fair and exhibition (April).

 Jacopone da Peppino, 5 Piazza Jacopone (tel. 075/882 366); *Umbria*, 13 Via S. Bonaventura (tel. 075/882 390).

Further to the south of Todi the fast E 7 crosses the Terni-Narni industrial basin. These two towns are gradually merging, hydroelectric power from the rivers Nera and Velino transforming the area into Umbria's 'little Ruhr'.

Tourists heading towards Perugia nowadays tend to take the motorway which bypasses both towns, but anyone with a special interest in art and architecture may find them worth a visit.

Terni Pop. 111,400

Terni's old centre boasts the 13th c. church of *S. Salvatore*, the richly ornamented *duomo*, and the ruins of a Roman *amphitheatre*. There are some noteworthy paintings of the Umbrian school (by Benozzo Gozzoli and others) in the *Pinacoteca* (Palazzo Manassei), while in the Gothic church of *S. Francesco* (Piazza S. Francesco) the *Cappella Paradisi* — the Paradisi family were podestà of the town — is decorated with frescos (1460) by Bartolomeo da Tomaso.

 Lago di Piediluco, Cascata delle Marmore.

 May Day Parade; water festival.

Narni Pop. 20,800

Proud and powerful on its hilltop Narni once rebelled against Barbarossa, withstood attack by the Hohenstaufen Frederick II, sided with the popes against the emperors, was later plundered by German mercenaries and now lives off the industries which have established themselves at its feet in the Terni basin below. The *Palazzo del Podestà*, consisting of three fortified tower-houses, and the

Loggia dei Priori are among the survivals from the past. The *Museo di S. Domenico* in a former church is now home to the town's art collection. There is a sweeping vista along the valley from up on the *Rocca*, the semi-derelict fortress.

 Caravan Park.

 Medieval tournament with midnight procession and jousting (May).

Narni provides a convenient point of departure for a detour through the hills to Amelia.

Amelia Pop. 11,100

Amelia — its pretty name derives from the former Roman stronghold of Ameria — is today still a favourite summer resort with the Romans, a hill town overlooking the valleys of the Tiber and its tributary the Nera. Although the tiny city state surrendered to the Papal States as early as 1307 it was still heavily plundered, and it has also suffered badly from earthquakes.

The marvellously well preserved town walls are best seen from the *Porta Romana*. Dating from the Roman period (4th c. BC) the walls are built from gigantic blocks (8 m high, 3.5 m thick) — without cement, yet still standing! The Via della Repubblica at first climbs quite gently up to the plain Gothic church of *SS. Filippo e Giacomo* in which some former noble and not quite so noble families have their tombs. It then becomes steeper, climbing still further to the *cathedral* (Romanesque in origin though the *campanile* provides the only clue). The inner courtyard of the *Palazzo Comunale* (Piazza Matteotti) is filled with beautiful marble fragments from the town's Roman and medieval past. If possible ask to be allowed into the delightful *theatre* (Via del Teatro) where 'Frederick Barbarossa laying siege to Amelia' is painted on the curtain (key at the council offices).

 Anita, 31 Via Roma (tel. 0 744/982 146).

From Amelia the SS 205 goes through the hills above the Tiber valley and on by a direct route to Orvieto. An alternative is to take one of the small cross-country roads to join up with the Autostrada del Sole.

At Assisi (see page 66) there is also an alternative to heading west for the Tiber valley. Continue south instead on the SS 75 to Spello (about 12 km).

Spello Pop. 7,600

With popes and emperors waging war against one another Spello, in common with all fortified towns in the Middle Ages, experienced difficult times. Constantly under threat from a seemingly endless chain of marauding knights and brigands the town was eventually plundered in 1529 by the troops of William of Orange. Soon afterwards its fortifications were razed and in 1583 the papacy took possession once more. Life then became quieter and more pious, a spirit still reflected today at Corpus Christi when the townsfolk hold their 'flower festival', covering the streets with a carpet of blossom. In autumn and winter, when the tourists have departed, the town also celebrates an olive festival and the *bruschetta* (garlic toast) festival.

 What to see

Walk through the *Borgo* with its steep winding alleyways and streets, between Gothic and Renaissance buildings. First of all you come to the *Porta Consolare* dating from Roman times, and the equally ancient *Porta Urbica* next to a battlemented medieval tower crowned with olive-trees. In the Via Cavour is the church of *S. Maria Maggiore* with the famous *Cappella Baglioni*. Walk across the beautifully tiled floor (the tiles made in Deruta — famous for its ceramics — in

1566) to admire the superb, recently restored frescos by Pinturicchio (1501). Although the town is tiny it still has its own art collection in the *Palazzo Comunale*.

Don't forget to visit the Roman *Porta Venere* (Gate of Venus), built during the reign of the Emperor Augustus, which is reached along the Via Torri di Properzio. And for anyone willing to walk a kilometre or so beyond the *Porta di Fontevecchia* there is the little Romanesque church of S. Claudio to be seen as well as the remains of the Roman *amphitheatre*.

 Il Molino, 6 Piazza Matteotti (tel. 0 742/651 305).

From Spello it is only a few minutes' drive on the SS 75 to Foligno.

Foligno Pop. 53,200

Foligno is one of three towns, the others being Bevagna and Montefalco, where to the eye at least the medieval heritage seems to have survived intact. Of the three Foligno is the most lively, being also the largest.

Set in the gentle and fertile Umbrian valley (Valle Umbra), girdled by hills and the Monti Martani, Foligno is nowadays encircled by a busy New Town. Even so, getting about presents no problems.

Since Roman times the town has stood at a crossing-point of several major routes, and during the artistic flowering of the Middle Ages it naturally drew cultural inspiration from further afield. Foligno's artists of course added embellishment of their own.

 What to see

With half a day given over to sightseeing make first for the *cathedral*. The Romanesque façade — 1133 is the date inscribed by Master Atto above the doorway — looks out over the Piazza del Duomo (cathedral square), centre of the old town. A second façade facing the Piazza della Repubblica

also has a very fine Romanesque doorway but was erected a generation later by the master builders Rodolfo and Binello. One of the heads in relief is said to represent Frederick Barbarossa.

Next to the cathedral stands the Gothic *Palazzo della Canonica*; opposite is the *Palazzo Comunale*, begun in the 13th c. but much altered since (the fortified tower is a 15th c. addition). The building of most interest however is the *Palazzo Trinci* on the north-east side of the Piazza. Over the years this suffered badly from earthquakes, and further damage was caused during the last war, but painstaking work has restored its noble appearance as well as its superb *Gothic staircase*. The Palazzo now makes a splendid setting for the *Municipal Archives*, the *Pinacoteca Comunale* and the *Archaeological Museum*. From time to time Foligno puts on exhibitions of modern art in this maze of halls, little rooms, staircases and arcades. While these cannot help but show how different today's art is from that of the past, they also show that our own art still has plenty to say.

Despite the abundance of churches — among them *S. Maria Infraportas* (frescos), *S. Nicolò* (fine doorway), *S. Giacomo* (with adjoining cloister), the *Oratorio della Nunziatella* (two works by Perugino) and the old Benedictine abbey of *S. Salvatore* (an architectural interplay of red and white, with three Gothic doorways) — none really comes into the category of 'absolute must'.

To walk from one church to another, however, is to pass almost without exception among well-preserved medieval buildings (although the signs of bombing during the last war have still not completely disappeared). In the Via dei Monasteri, No. 16 is the so-called *Monastero delle Contesse* (the Convent of the Countesses); all too often the daughters of the high-born had little option but to enter upon a religious life behind closed doors. For a long time the nuns here owned a work by Raphael, the

Madonna di Foligno, which they steadfastly refused to part with at any price, not even to Queen Christina of Sweden. Then Napoleon came and stole it. When the picture was returned to Italy in 1816 the Vatican kept it for its own *pinacoteca*, thus depriving Foligno of its treasure.

 Umbria.

 Giostra della Quintana (2nd Sunday in September): medieval jousting.

 Da Remo, 11 Via C. Battisti (tel. 0 742/50 079).

Foligno is the starting point for a short circular tour, with Bevagna the first destination.

Bevagna Pop. 4,500

Bevagna is still something of a secret. Few foreigners manage to find their way to this ancient little town at the foot of verdant hills, at the point where the Timia joins the Clitunno and the Teverone. The Umbrians settled here long before the Romans arrived; the latter left their mark by establishing a provisioning-post and brickworks. In the Middle Ages Bevagna's allegiance was to the papacy and it remained firmly under the protection of the Church until modern times.

Since the 13th c. the town has been enclosed by 2 km of walls pierced by six gates, some of the stone for these walls having been taken from Roman buildings. A neat semicircle of houses preserves the line of the former Roman *amphitheatre*. Enthroned above wide steps in the Piazza Garibaldi is the square-towered 13th c. church of *S. Francesco*. Bevagna's patron saint, Vincenzo, has been deprived of his church, however; it is now a cinema. Fragments of Roman marble — reliefs, bits of statues and other ornamentation — can be seen on many of the buildings.

Rising up between more modest medieval buildings on the Piazza Silvestri is the Gothic *Palazzo dei Consoli*, its wide external staircase leading in to a most beautiful theatre. To the right of the Palazzo stands *S. Silvestro*, a glorious Romanesque church built by Master Binello in 1195 ('signed' with a marble inscription above the entrance). He also built the nearby church of *S. Michele* with its altogether more grandiose façade.

 Pian di Boccio.

 Del Cacciatore da Nina, 5 Piazza Garibaldi (tel. 0 742/62 161).

Ex Around Bevagna the countryside is peppered with pilgrimage churches and monasteries including *Madonna delle Grazie* (2–3 km south-east), *Convento dell'Annunziata* (3 km north-east) and *S. Fortunato* just outside Montefalco. Montefalco itself is the next port of call.

Montefalco Pop. 5,500

Peering down from a height of 500 m over the plain of the rivers Topino and Clitunno this small medieval town is sometimes called the 'balcony of Umbria'. Even those who are not much interested in its famous frescos are thus promised plenty to delight the eye. As it happens, however, its papal governors endowed Montefalco with a particular treasure and the *Museo* in the former church of *S. Francesco* demands a visit, no matter how brief. The entire fresco cycle in the Gothic apse was painted by Benozzo Gozzoli (1452). The *Storie di S. Francesco* are told in a series of truly enchanting pictures, their simplicity of style being reminiscent of Fra Angelico. It was through these frescos that almost every Umbrian artist of the Renaissance period was introduced to the new Tuscan style, and Montefalco became the source of the greatest inspiration to painting in central Italy.

As well as the churches of *S. Agostino*

Fresco by Benozzo Gozzoli, Montefalco

and *S. Maria Maddalena*, the *Palazzo Comunale* with its beautiful council chambers should also be seen. The climb to the top of its battlemented tower is rewarded with one of Italy's finest panoramas — you can see Spoleto, Campello, Trevi, Foligno, Spello, Assisi, Perugia, Bevagna, Gualdo Cattaneo and a myriad little hamlets and castles against the unparalleled backdrop of the Umbrian Apennines and the Abruzzi mountains. Umbria lies spread at your feet.

From Montefalco drive back to Foligno. From Foligno take the road via Trevi and the Fonti del Clitunno to Spoleto.

Spoleto Pop. 38,000

Spoleto is wonderfully unspoiled. Over the centuries the medieval character of its architecture was preserved even though the town was gradually losing its impor-

tance as a papal stronghold. When in due course peace reigned and a condition little short of inertia descended upon the Papal States, Spoleto, unlike most towns in Umbria, continued to enjoy a certain prestige, a fact reflected in later buildings like the little *Caio Melisso Theatre*. Through the happy circumstance of being 'discovered' by Giancarlo Menotti, founder of the *Festival dei Due Mondi*, Spoleto has once more come into its own.

 What to see

Cathedral: The *duomo*, a Romanesque building with a lovely façade, is the very heart of the town. From the Via del Duomo running a little way above, wide steps lead down into the spacious cathedral square with its surrounding palazzi. The cathedral itself was erected in the 13th c. on the site of an earlier church razed to the ground by the Emperor Barbarossa (Spoleto was one of the most fiercely contested of all cities in the conflict between the Holy Roman Empire and the papacy). In the interior of the cathedral (presbytery, apse) the delicate shades of Fra Filippo Lippi's enormous fresco (1467–69) immediately capture the eye. There are frescos by Pinturicchio in the chapel.

La Rocca: After looking round the cathedral climb up to the fortress — now a prison — which sits glowering over the town. This substantial stronghold with six robust towers was built on the orders of Cardinal Albornoz, the medieval Church's most irascible warlord. He intended it as a secure retreat for the popes following the papacy's return from Avignon. The fortress stands directly above the Tessino gorge which is spanned by a bridge, the *Ponte delle Torri*.

Piazza Campello: Back in the town centre head for the *Palazzo Comunale* and the adjacent *Palazzo Campello*, the first of

Ponte delle Torri, Spoleto

which contains the *Pinacoteca*. From here a picturesque maze of alleyways leads to more churches (about a dozen) and palazzi. A little further down from the Palazzo Comunale there is a 1st c. Roman house (*casa romana*) to be seen. Festival concerts are held in what was originally the Roman *amphitheatre* (and was later

Romanesque façade, Spoleto Cathedral

turned into a fortress by King Totila). Also interesting are remains of the Roman walls and a Roman bridge (*Ponte Sanguinario*).

S. Pietro: The church of *S. Pietro* stands just outside the town on the southern exit road. It has a most unusual façade decorated with animal reliefs (13th c.) and is well worth seeing. The interior is being restored.

Festival of the Two Worlds (June/July).

La Cantina, 10a Via Filetteria (tel. 0 743/44 475); *Il Tartufo*, 24 Piazza Garibaldi (tel. 0 743/40 236).

Before taking the main road some 30 km south to the industrial area around Terni and Narni (see page 71), make a detour into the Nera valley to Norcia and Cascia (see page 78).

The Nera valley

Exploring the Nera valley is a kind of pilgrimage into the furthest corner of Umbria, which is rich in stories of saints and miracles.

Once outside Spoleto the SS 395 at first climbs easily towards the Passo del Cerro (called at its highest point Forca di Cerro) before becoming a true mountain road. Dense chestnut-forests cover the steep hillsides and the distant views become increasingly majestic. Far below in the Nera valley are the little poplar-bordered fields of the first small town, Piedipaterno, where the road joins the SS 209 (to Visso). At *Triponzo* pause to inspect one of ancient Rome's technical marvels, a tunnel bored through a massive wall of limestone. Three mountain streams converge here, the three bridges giving Triponzo its name. All were frequently fought over in the Middle Ages.

Drive on in the direction of Serravalle (narrow valley, as the name implies) to reach Norcia after 17 km.

Spoleto — a modern fairy-tale

Twenty-five years ago the little town of Spoleto lay in a time-warp. Anyone with ambition packed his bags and headed north. A once eventful and turbulent history, when the town ruled over a Lombard duchy, was long forgotten. There was a great deal of poverty and little hope. All in all the past seemed like a curse.

One day a young man arrived on his travels. It was just a coincidence that he turned off the main highway to have a look at the old hill town. He saw narrow, steep streets between handsome, once noble houses. He saw an impressive cathedral and facing it a spacious, slightly cambered square. He saw a solid, silent castle planted on the hilltop, and a deep ravine, audaciously bridged across to wooded slopes with sleepy hermitages. All this gave him an idea: he wanted to turn this medieval 'sleeping beauty' into a festival town. He wanted to make music here, his own and that of others. For he was a composer, a composer who had achieved early fame, especially in distant America, and had become rich from his operas.

Giancarlo Menotti did not want to live in America, preferring always to return to his native Italy. He wanted if he could to unite the two. So it was that he conceived the idea of his *Festival dei Due Mondi*, Festival of the Two Worlds. Many wealthy people were excited by his idea and were persuaded to give generous support. To begin with only a few music-lovers were aware of the summer festival, which culminated in a great open-air concert on the cathedral square conducted by a young maestro, Thomas Shippers. But word soon spread. Festivals however need a great deal of money and Giancarlo Menotti was often on the verge of despair, tempted to unburden himself of the demanding and exhausting role of fairytale prince.

But nobody, not the state, nor any other authority, volunteered relief. What would become of the town that had only just awoken? What would become of the many little restaurants, the small hotels, the shops and art galleries newly opened in the ancient alleyways, and which had drawn the migrant townspeople home to work in Spoleto?

Giancarlo Menotti held on from one year to the next, and Spoleto became more famous, more confident, and better provided with hotels. Now it plays host to more than the opera, the ballet, the theatre and the many guests from home and abroad during the festival months of June and July. It has become a popular conference venue for the rest of the year too. Among the groups who meet there are *Italia Nostra*, Italy's environmentalists. Having always been rather a voice in the wilderness the society has gained new heart from what has happened to Spoleto. In April there is a Medieval Studies Conference. There are organ concerts from April to June, an experimental opera festival in September and a large art exhibition in October. The alleys are no longer rutted, the houses no longer badly weathered — all is now carefully restored, and the town's medieval heritage remains intact. Its buildings are lived in and everywhere is alive. Today Spoleto can stand on its own feet and is a place of renown. Giancarlo Menotti is more than a freeman of the town — he is in effect its adored patron saint.

Norcia Pop. 4,700

Norcia is the birthplace of St Benedict of Nursia (480–546) and his twin sister St Scholastica. Benedict effectively founded European monasticism in founding the Benedictine order. The extremely ancient, wonderfully pretty little town, Roman in origin, was still very populous in the Middle Ages, and remains completely surrounded by very solid town walls. Many of the buildings, however, suffered badly from an earthquake in 1978.

 Dal Francese, 16 Via Riguardati (tel. 0 743/816 290); *Grotta Azzurra*, 12 Via Alfieri (tel. 0 743/816 513).

Ex New life has been brought to the area by a growing stream of tourists, including those attracted in winter to the ski slopes of *Forca Canapine*. The landscape is ravishingly beautiful, especially in the fertile plain of S. Scolastica, while hidden away on the hilltops all around are little pilgrimage churches and old monasteries. There are, too, delightful views of the Monti Sibillini to be enjoyed. For climbers there is *Monte Vettore* (2,476 m and not to be attempted without a mountain guide), brooding over the magnificent upland plain of Castelluccio. Go back via Serravalle to the SS 320, turning south onto the road to Cascia (12 km).

Cascia Pop. 3,300

This picturesque little place of pilgrimage clings to the side of a hill at the furthest edge of Umbria. Its patron saint, St Rita, is protector and comforter of harassed housewives, having entered a nunnery late in life after suffering all manner of family vicissitudes. On her saint's day (May 22nd) and at Ferragosto (mid-August) the village streets are crammed with coach-borne pilgrims.

 Feast of St Rita (May 22nd), torchlight procession.

 Cursula, 3 Via Cavour (tel. 0 743/76 206).

Ex If you wish to head across the regional border into nearby Lazio, the shortest route goes through the Abruzzi mountains. But a special treat awaits those retracing their steps and returning on the Triponzo road in the direction of Terni.

Abbazia di San Pietro in Valle is an abbey only a short distance from the road, though it is not that easy to find! Almost at kilometre-post 22, immediately behind a cluster of houses called Sambucheto, a small road off to the right climbs steeply to a height of 364 m. Few places can be as blessed as this abbey with such magical scenery and such eloquent art. Its frescos date from the time of the Lombard duchy of Spoleto when painting turned away from the Byzantine style in search of new directions (end of the 13th c.). If there doesn't happen to be a wedding party here you will probably have the monastery grounds to yourself, the peace broken only by the sound of birds.

If you are driving along this same road on a Sunday, you will notice buses parked by the roadside at a spot about 7 km before Terni. They will have brought trippers and schoolchildren to see the *Cascate delle Marmore*, a waterfall produced as the River Velino is 'unleashed' to plunge over a 165-m-high wall of marble into the River Nera below. It is allowed to do so only on Sundays, being harnessed for the rest of the week to generate electricity for the factories in Terni and Narni— Umbria's 'little Ruhr' (see page 71). The waterfall incidentally has always been artificial. Almost 2,000 years ago the ancient Romans diverted the Velino because it flooded the fertile plains.

From Orvieto to Volterra

Nowhere is it easier to forget than in Orvieto that Italy is a peninsula with thousands of kilometres of coastline. High, broad mountain ridges insulate the interior of central Italy from the sea. It is these same hills and valleys that cause the air traveller flying over them to be amazed at how harsh and mountainous Italy looks, how lacking in fertile plains. Nowadays there is little difficulty in getting to towns and villages that only a few decades ago suffered by their remoteness, despite often being known the world over.

Construction of the Autostrada del Sole at the end of the 1950s brought the decisive breach in the wall of comparative isolation. Setting out from Orvieto our route heads north-west through Siena (and other towns on the way) until it gradually approaches the coast at Pisa. There is much depopulated countryside to be seen along this stretch of road, and many forest-covered slopes, but also the distinctive crumbly soil of Siena; farms lie abandoned in the hills but, in turn, land accessible to machinery is newly under cultivation. The expansion of viticulture has helped to put the whole area's economy back on its feet, supported by all manner of small businesses and craft industries — and last but not least by the tourists who are made so welcome.

Orvieto Pop. 22,800

Orvieto, looking for all the world like an island (which indeed it was in prehistoric times), stands on a flat-topped lava outcrop 300 m above the broad valley of the River Paglia just where it runs into the Tiber. Crowded onto its hilltop, the town has managed to preserve its medieval character.

 Around the cathedral

Orvieto's heart is its wonderfully colourful cathedral, on which work started in the 13th c. Building was still in progress at the end of the 15th c. and was continued by successive generations. The cathedral is still the centre of the town's community life.

Having made the twisting climb up to the Old Town from Orvieto Scalo (the Etruscan necropolis is off to the right at the foot of the cliff) sit down on a bench in the cathedral square.

Striped in black basalt and yellowy limestone, embellished with sculptures, mosaics, columns and stone tracery, the glorious façade resembles a three-tiered triptych. Try not to miss the opportunity on a Sunday of seeing the cathedral floodlit —

it seems even more unreal than in daylight. The best time of day to view the interior on the other hand is in late afternoon; see especially the *Cappella Nuova* with its beautiful frescos by Luca Signorelli. Even Michelangelo found inspiration in Signorelli's *End of the World* when

Cathedral façade, Orvieto

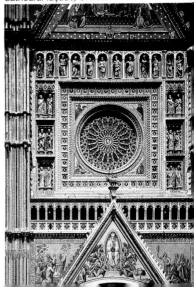

working on the Sistine Chapel in Rome.

The story of the building of Orvieto's cathedral goes back to the *Miracle of Bolsena*. The miracle, depicted in a painting by Raphael in the Vatican, is said to have occurred in the 13th c. and involved a Bohemian monk gripped by doubts about the presence of Christ in the host of the Eucharist. His doubts vanished when on this occasion a drop of blood fell from the host. Ever since then Orvieto has celebrated the miracle with a solemn procession at the feast of Corpus Christi.

To the side of the cathedral are two palaces both containing museums. The cathedral museum is in the *Palazzo Soliano* and the archaeological museum in the *Palazzo Papale*. The latter name — 'papal palace' — is a reminder that the popes used this hilltop town as a place of refuge (barricading off all access to the rock plateau). After Rome was cruelly plundered by the emperor's mercenaries (1527) Pope Clement VII even sank a famous well, the *Pozzo di San Patrizio*, to safeguard Orvieto's water supplies in case of siege. A huge circular shaft (5 m in diameter) was dug 200 m down into the tuff strata till it struck ground-water in the marl beneath.

The well is actually something of a masterpiece, created by Antonio da Sangallo, the papal architect, and others. Two spiral staircases each with 250 steps are cut into the tufa — one for going down, one for coming up — enabling donkeys to carry water from the depths day and night, a supply so seemingly inexhaustible that even today people refer to anyone especially generous or rich as the 'Pozzo di San Patrizio'. From the bottom of the shaft the stars can be seen plainly even in the daytime.

Orvieto is now an important commercial distribution centre, the New Town in the valley being served by both the railway and the Autostrada del Sole. On the slopes

Orvieto, the cathedral

of the surrounding hills particularly good white wine is produced. It is served in the many hostelries, which are good but not cheap.

 Feast of Corpus Christi: procession (historical dress); Dove Festival (Whit Sunday).

 Dell'Ancora, 5 Via Piazza del Popolo (tel. 0 763/42 766); *Maurizio*, 78 Via del Duomo (tel. 0 763/41 114); *Morino*, 37 Via Garibaldi (tel. 0 763/41 952).

Follow the Autostrada del Sole north from Orvieto as far as the Chianciano Terme exit. From here take the SS 146 to Montepulciano.

Montepulciano Pop. 14,200

Montepulciano is perched high (605 m) on a hill between the valley of the Orcia on one side and the Chiana valley on the other, commanding a magnificent panorama. Its major buildings are those of a Renaissance town of Florentine influence, but the challenge of steep, narrow medieval streets and alleys must be met before reaching them. The elongated town is in fact Etruscan in origin.

Up until the 17th c. Montepulciano was a lively cultural centre, but thereafter it lay forgotten in a rural backwater until ten or so years ago, when the composer Hans Werner Henze organised a summer music festival in the town. The lovely piazza on the hilltop, flanked by the *Palazzo Comunale*, the *Palazzo Contucci* and the *Palazzo Tarugi*, provides a perfect setting, and the young musicians and music-lovers drawn here from all over the world have the many churches in and around Montepulciano to enjoy. The local people have welcomed the strangers in their midst — like Spoleto, Montepulciano was in need of its fairytale musical prince.

 Cantiere Internazionale d'Arte (music festival).

From Montepulciano continue on the SS 146 to the little town of Pienza.

Pienza Pop. 2,400

Pienza represents the realisation of a dream. Pope Pius II (Aeneas Silvius Piccolomini) — that most worldly and humanistic of prelates — aspired to create an archetypal Renaissance town near his modest family castle at Corsignano. Hence the name Pienza, conferred on the town by papal bull in 1459.

 A walk round the Old Town

Standing on the *Piazza Pio II* with its important-looking palazzi and cathedral you could be forgiven for thinking that you were at the heart of a great town. Work started in 1459 under the architect Bernardo Rossellino, though twelve houses and the church of *S. Francesco* were commissioned from a number of other master builders. Not satisfied even with this the Pope forced his cardinals to erect sumptuous palaces as well. When Pius and Rossellino both died within a short time of each other Pienza was left unfinished, although today what they created seems quite perfect. The travertine *cathedral*, a hall church with three lovely doorways and a *campanile*, has a richly decorated interior which is always filled with light. There is a masterpiece by Vecchietta in the fourth chapel and a beautiful font in the crypt below the apse. The plain Renaissance building (*Casa dei Canonici*) next to the cathedral is the *Museo della Cattedrale*, where there are also works of art brought from other churches for safe keeping. To the left of the museum is the *bishop's palace*, built by Cardinal Borgia at the Pope's insistence. Opposite the cathedral stands the old *Palazzo Comunale* — unfortunately heavily restored — and at one end of the piazza can be seen the rusticated stonework of the *Palazzo Piccolomini*, whose architect (Rossellino) was clearly inspired by the Palazzo Ruccellai in Florence. This marvellously elegant building has an arcaded inner court, surpassed in beauty only by the adjacent 'hanging garden', from where there is a superb vista across the Orcia valley to Monte Amiata. To the right of the Palazzo is a small building which the Pope had to have added later; in his intoxicated pursuit of perfection the architect had neglected to include a kitchen in his plans!

After visiting Pienza head west again on the SS 146, negotiating its bends for about 10 km until it joins the SS 2 (Via Cassia) — a good but also very winding road — near S. Quirico. Turn north in the direction of Buonconvento to Siena, a distance of some 44 km.

Siena Pop. 61,300

Siena is the noblest of all the Tuscan towns — and knows it! Nowhere else is there such a depth of civic pride and awareness of tradition — no folk festival has had to be revived here, and the celebrations are if anything more splendid today. The different districts or *contrade* have always spent the entire year arguing excitedly about the *Palio*, the extraordinary medieval horse-race run in the scallop-shaped piazza known as the *Campo* (field). It creates both rivalries and bonds. And yet this twice-yearly display of horsemanship is over in three minutes! The preparations and the post mortems on the other hand last for days — in fact they never really stop.

A walk round the town

Piazza del Campo: Siena cannot really be seen in a single day, but sightseeing should anyway start in the *Campo*, now as always the centre of community life. It owes its unique shape, a shallow concavity, to the convergence here of the three hills on which Siena is built. As early as 1347 this magnificent oval was paved in an elaborate fan of patterned brick, and in front of the supremely elegant Gothic *Palazzo Pubblico* (1297–1310), with its bold tower (*Torre del Mangia*), Siena's eventful history has been played out, the encircling palaces providing an unequalled backdrop for public gatherings, insurrections, spectacles and contests. Strangers and Sienese alike lounge by the *Fonte Gaia*, a marble fountain decorated with reliefs by Jacopo della Quercia (only copies, the originals having been removed to the Palazzo Pubblico). The *Cappella di Piazza* at the foot of the tall tower was built in 1352, in fulfilment of a vow made during an epidemic of the plague.

Palazzo Pubblico: While the first floor of the *Palazzo Pubblico* is given over to the *Museo Civico*, the Palazzo's greatest trea-

Above: View over Siena
Right: The Palio, Siena

sures are the walls of the rooms themselves; the *Maestà* for instance, a large
fresco of the Madonna and Child by
Simone Martini (1315), graces the left-
hand wall of the *Sala del Mappamondo*.

The superb wall- and ceiling-paintings
depicting scenes from Siena's history are
far too numerous to allow more than a
mention of the most important of them.
Still in the Sala del Mappamondo, on the
short wall above the entrance, there is an
equestrian portrait of *Guidoriccio da
Fogliano*, commander-in-chief of the
Sienese army, leaving to besiege Monte-
massi — a delightfully original work by
Simone Martini (1328). In the *Sala della*

Piazza del Campo

Pace on the right, once the council chamber, the ideology of the ruling Signori is captured in Ambrogio Lorenzetti's great allegorical compositions (1338–40) which cover three walls: *Buon Governo*, 'Good Government' (on the wall opposite the windows), shows the ruler with figures representing generosity, moderation, justice, prudence, strength, and peace (*la pace*) — a wondrous figure in white, posed as if at ease on a sofa. *Effetti del Buon Governo* on the right-hand wall depicts the effects of good government on the city and the country, the effects of bad government being shown on the wall opposite (which has unfortunately deteriorated badly). There is nothing of such beauty, or on so grand a scale, more revealing of life in a medieval city than Lorenzetti's frescos. They are the first works of this size to have been devoted to a secular rather than a religious theme.

There is a great deal more to see in this venerable old palace, and still more from the tower, if you climb the 400 steps.

Alleyways off the Campo (e.g. Chiasso del Bargello) lead immediately into Siena's main thoroughfare, at this point called the Via di Città. The *Chigiana* academy of music (in the *Palazzo Chigi Saracini* to the left) is famous for the courses held for both Italians and foreigners, usually in July and August.

Cathedral district: Continue walking along the Via di Città (the distances are not great) to the Gothic *Palazzo del Capitano del Popolo*, now the home of the university's faculty of economics. From here (left corner) the splendid cathedral square is already visible: the long façade of the old *Spedale di S. Maria della Scala* (still a hospital), the *bishop's palace* and the huge marble *duomo*. From its very earliest beginnings in 1196 the cathedral has had an eventful history. A *duomo nuovo* (enlarging the existing building) was begun but never completed, as the open walls on the right of the piazza testify. The plague and political adversity forced the Sienese to abandon their planned colossus, intended to outshine the cathedral of the rival city of Florence. 'Unfinished' it may be, but the existing cathedral is still endowed with an abundance of riches, including its colourful, liberally ornamented *marble façade* combining Romanesque and

Cathedral façade, Siena

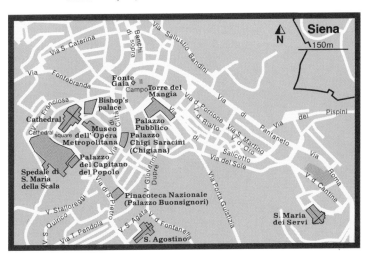

Palazzo Pubblico, Siena

Detail, Siena Cathedral

Gothic styles, and the Romanesque *campanile*. The breathtaking interior (cruciform, three-aisled) is about 90 m long and 25 m wide, the black and white striped stonework giving rise to a shadowy light-dark effect. The floor consists of 56 engraved and inlaid marble panels which in themselves represent a chapter in the history of art and allegory. It is impossible to do justice to the wealth of magnificent ornamentation with which the interior abounds. The marble *pulpit* (1266–68) by Nicola Pisano marks with its stylistic innovations the full flowering of Italian Gothic sculpture. The *Cappella di S. Giovanni Battista* (Renaissance in style) is decorated with fine frescos by Pinturicchio. It is in the *Libreria Piccolomini* however that the spirit of humanism shines out most strongly, especially in Pinturicchio's superb cycle of frescos which provides such fitting adornment to the library of Pope Pius II.

Leaving the cathedral through a door-way in the unfinished section you reach some steps, down which is the *battistero* (baptistry) with the famous font by Jacopo della Quercia (1417). Mount the steps again to look at the loveliest of all Sienese paintings in the *Museo dell'Opera Metropolitana* next to the cathedral. Don't allow the collection of masterpieces by Giovanni Pisano, Simone Martini, Pietro Lorenzetti and Jacopo della Quercia to divert you from the incomparable *Maestà* by Duccio di Buoninsegna (first floor). After years of restoration this great altarpiece (1308–11) can be seen in all its glory again. Against a gold background the Madonna is depicted enthroned between angels and saints. There is a moving inscription on the step below the throne: 'Holy Mother of God, be Thou peace for Siena, be Thou life for Duccio who has painted Thee so.' When the work was complete the whole population of Siena gathered in triumphal procession to escort it to the cathedral.

Anyone spending several days in Siena should visit the *Pinacoteca Nazionale* (in the Palazzo Buonsignori); it has numerous Late Gothic and other paintings. To get to the Palazzo go along the Via di Città and turn left to reach 29 Via S. Pietro.

Churches

Siena's treasures are still not exhausted! There is Pietro Lorenzetti's famous painting *The Slaughter of the Innocents* in the 'servants' church', *S. Maria dei Servi*; there are more frescos by Lorenzetti in the church of *S. Francesco*, and still more (along with paintings by other artists) in the *Cappella Piccolomini* in *S. Agostino*. The winding streets, through which you can stroll at leisure since most are pedestrianised, also boast many superb palazzi.

The skyline of San Gimignano

 Horse-racing on the Piazza del Campo (July 2nd and August 15th).

 Da Guido, 7 Vicolo Pier Pettinaio (tel. 0 577/280 042); *Antica Trattoria Botteganova*, Strada Chiantigiana (tel. 0 577/284 230).

After Siena head for S. Gimignano and Volterra, both supremely beautiful towns. Having followed the SS 2 (Via Cassia) to Colle di Val d'Elsa (c. 25 km) turn off onto the SS 68. Here there are two possibilities: one is to turn right after a few kilometres in the direction of Bibbiano (12 km to S. Gimignano), the other to continue as far as Castel S. Gimignano, turning right there for S. Gimignano itself, a drive of 22 km via Monte Oliveto.

San Gimignano Pop. 7,400

S. Gimignano's skyline is like that of a small, medieval New York — all skyscrapers! From the top of the *Palazzo del Popolo* a count shows thirteen of the old towers (built by the town's rival families) still standing — there are thought to have once been about sixty. The town itself, set on a gently sloping hill, is perfect for tourists: everything worth seeing can be seen in a day exploring on foot. The cathedral square is the most rewarding part.

 What to see

The cathedral has lovely frescos by Barna and Ghirlandaio and there are paintings from the 13th to the 17th c. in the *Pinacoteca* in the *Palazzo del Popolo*. Next to the Palazzo del Popolo stand the *Palazzo del Podestà* and the *Torri* (towers built by rival families). Away from the town centre, the church of *S. Agostino* is decorated with frescos by Gozzoli, Pollaiuolo and Benedetto da Maiano.

Having walked up to the town's ruined fortress you will probably find yourself surrounded by fellow tourists. So for something rather more out-of-the-way go to the *Porta S. Jacopo*, a gate in the medieval town walls, and from there along to the *Porta alle Fonti* (well gate), where sheep as well as clothes used to be scrubbed clean under the ten arches.

San Gimignano

 S. Gimignano carnival.

 Le Terrazze, Piazza della Cisterna (tel. 0 577/940 328).

From S. Gimignano it is best to rejoin the SS 68 which, though winding, brings you quickly to Volterra. If you drive to Volterra direct from the Autostrada del Sole, turn off at the Poggibonsi exit.

Volterra Pop. 13,900

Having been one of the most powerful Etruscan cities — *Velathri* — Volterra possesses one of the most famous Etruscan museums (700 cinerary urns made from alabaster and tufa, ceramics, bronzes, etc.). Stendhal, d'Annunzio and D.H. Lawrence have all written about it.

 What to see

The *Museo Etrusco* is located in the *Palazzo Guarnacci* (15 Via Don Minzoni), about four minutes' walk from the square in front of the *Palazzo dei Priori* which is the centre of town. In the 12th c. Volterra was already an autonomous city, though locked in continual conflict with Florence. The Florentines were mainly interested in the nearby alum pits which were indispensable for their tanneries. White and coloured alabaster, Volterra's other natural resource, remains a valuable asset, for export and for use by local craftsmen.

The town's architecture is its greatest asset of all, however — medieval towers, dark and high, and town walls and gates, some dating back to Etruscan and Roman times. The *Palazzo dei Priori* is Tuscany's oldest town hall (1208–54). The *Galleria Pittorica* inside the Palazzo has an important picture by Luca Signorelli (1491) among its paintings. Set to one side on the square is the 13th c. Romanesque cathedral — enlarged later in the Pisan style — in the interior of which (second chapel) is a very early painted wooden sculpture (mid-14th c.). Opposite stands the octagonal *battistero* (baptistry), faced with coloured marble.

Volterra is in danger of crumbling away. The hill on which it stands (550 m) is slowly breaking up. The *balze* (deeply eroded gullies in the clay) are most in evidence on the west side.

Of the two routes from Volterra to Pisa the more direct is the SS 439 which joins the main Firenze–Mare road at Pontedera.

The second possibility is to stay on the SS 68 until near Cecina where two further options present themselves. One is to turn north at the junction with the SS 206 (to Pisa via Collesalvetti), the other to go on as far as Cecina and the SS 1 (Via Aurelia), following the coast to Pisa via Livorno. The latter route is somewhat longer but slightly easier.

No tour through the heart of Tuscany and Umbria could end more fittingly than with the sight of Pisa's *Torre Pendente* once again.

Useful things to know

Before you go

Climate

The climate is more distinctly 'Mediterranean' on the coast than inland, which means that the coast is cooler in summer than the Florentine basin or the Chiana valley for example, with more likelihood of a breeze. In winter on the other hand the coast is warmer and drier. During their dry summer, temperatures in Florence, Arezzo and Perugia average about 25°C/78°F, but at higher altitudes, in places such as Vallombrosa (1,000 m), they reach only 17°C/62°F. Average winter temperatures in Livorno, Pisa and Florence range from 4°C/40°F to 7°C/44°F, but in the mountains they hover around freezing or below. Rainy spells are more typical of spring and autumn (April/May and October/November) than winter. Snow is almost entirely confined to the mountains, the ski season in the Apuan Alps and the Apennines (Abetone) running from December to March. At this time of year mist quite often lingers in the valleys, unless dispersed by the *tramontana*, the cold north-east wind which brings sub-zero temperatures in its train (usually for about three days). Florence, Arezzo, Perugia, etc. are liable to feel its effects.

Geography

Tuscany and Umbria are predominantly hilly and mountainous. Plains are found only in parts of the coastal strip bordering the Tyrrhenian Sea, in the river valleys of the Arno, Tiber and Ombrone, and in the Chiana valley; even then they amount to less than a tenth of the total area. The Apennines run right through the two regions from north to south, forming a wide, hard backbone to the area which, for all its division into separate valleys, has a certain geographical uniformity overall.

The term 'Pre-Apennines' is used to describe the chain of uplands which runs from close to the Tyrrhenian Sea inland to Montecatini in the north and Chiusi in the south, with spurs forming the islands of the Tuscan archipelago. The precise extent of the Alpi Apuane and Monti Metalliferi ('metal mountains') is still a matter of disagreement among geographers. Their scenic charm however is undisputed. Neither the Apennines nor the Apuan Alps are as high as the real Alps, being under 2,000 m, but they are impressive enough when seen from the coastal lowlands or the valleys. The valleys often form deep, narrow clefts and in many areas (e.g. around Volterra and Siena) the clay earth of the hills shows distinct signs of erosion.

The rivers of Tuscany are modest in length and most carry little water. The course of the Arno is 240 km long, that of the Ombrone only 160 km. Since the terrain is not very porous water levels in the rivers relate directly to the rainfall at any particular time: they are low in dry seasons but with heavy precipitation can quickly become high, often dangerously so, and can wash away large quantities of soil — witness the dreadful flooding in Florence in 1966.

Umbria is dominated by the Tiber, the only large river in central Italy. It flows through more than 200 km of Umbrian countryside, a distance amounting to half its course, and is fed by many small tributaries, the most important of which is the Nera, into which the Velito flows. The Fonti del Clitunno are a unique feature, water pouring from underground springs at 1,300 litres a second forming a delightful lake.

Umbria's lakes are really no more than pools despite their size. The Lago di Massaciuccoli is only 4.4 m deep, the lake at Montepulciano barely over 3 m; the huge Lake Trasimene, 6 m at its deepest point, is prone to recede to such an extent that it threatens to become a swamp. Only the little Lago di Piediluco reaches the respectable depth of almost 20 m.

Getting to Tuscany and Umbria

By air: Tuscany and Umbria are served by airports at Pisa (*Galileo Galilei*) and Florence (*Perentola*). There are connecting flights to both from Milan as well as direct (scheduled and charter) flights from abroad. It is also possible to fly to Rome (*Leonardo da Vinci/Fiumicino*), continuing the journey to Tuscany by coach.

By rail: There is a direct rail service from London Victoria to Florence.

By road: It is a very long way by car from Britain to Tuscany, and most motorists are thus effectively limited to motorway travel. Car sleeper services will shorten the journey time; information from the French or Belgian state railways.

Itineraries can be supplied on application to the RAC Routes Department at Croydon, tel. 081 686 0088 (address on page 94).

Immigration and customs regulations

Customs: Luggage and personal effects including e.g. 2 cameras and 10 films, a video camera and 10 films, portable radio, portable musical instrument, portable tape-recorder, television set, typewriter and binoculars may be taken into Italy duty free. Goods of no commercial value such as food and gifts also incur no duty.

The usual allowances for goods obtained duty paid in the EC apply on entry and departure: 300 cigarettes or 75 cigars or 400 g tobacco; 1.5 litres of spirits over 22% or 3 litres of spirits up to 22%, and 5 litres of wine; 1 kg coffee, 200 g tea, 75 g perfume.

Non-EC visitors should check allowances with their tour operator.

Duty-free allowances: 200 cigarettes or 50 cigars or 250 g tobacco; 1 litre of spirits over 22% or 2 litres of spirits up to 22%, and 2 litres of wine.

Travel documents: British visitors to Italy require only a valid passport or a British Visitor's Passport. US and Canadian visitors also require only a passport. A visa is needed only for stays exceeding 3 months.

Motorists are advised to obtain an international 'green card' insurance certificate to avoid lengthy discussions at police controls. In addition they need a valid driving licence and registration documents.

During your stay

Camping

The Italian camping and caravan club *Federazione Italiana del Campeggio* (Casella Postale 649, 50100 Firenze) publishes a camping guide every year. A list of the major campsites can also be obtained from ENIT offices (see page 94).

Currency

There are no restrictions on the import of foreign currency into Italy though the amount taken out on leaving the country may not exceed the amount taken in. There is no restriction on the import of Italian money; a maximum of 500,000 lire may be taken out.

You can obtain up to 300,000 lire with one Eurocheque.

Currently in circulation are 5, 10, 20, 50, 100, 200 and 500 lire coins, and notes in denominations of 1,000, 2,000, 5,000, 10,000, 50,000 and 100,000 lire. The 50,000 and 100,000 lire notes are legal tender only in Italy, not abroad. The grooved telephone tokens (*gettoni*) can also be tendered in lieu of cash (200 lire).

Exchange rates are published in the national press, or can be obtained from banks.

Electricity

The voltage in most hotels is 110 or 220 volts (you can see which from the light bulbs). Italian sockets (*presa*) do not normally take the standard UK or US plugs so an adaptor (*adattore*) is needed (obtainable from hotel reception or electrical shops, or, better still, before departure).

Hotels and pensions

Italy has five categories of hotel: luxury, and first down to fourth class. Pensions are categorised from 1 to 3. These give only a rough indication of standards and often a category 2 hotel will prove as good as if not better than one in the first category. The overnight, half-board and full-board tariffs must be displayed in the hotel room. Many hotels offer reductions for children.

Insurance

UK citizens travelling in Italy are covered for minor illnesses under an EC agreement (a form E111 should be obtained from the DSS or a post office before leaving home). The equivalent Italian health department (INAM) will exchange this form for a treatment voucher. It is also advisable however to take out additional medical insurance.

Comprehensive travel insurance covering third-party liability, health, accident and luggage is available from travel agencies and at airports. British motorists may obtain RAC Eurocover insurance from RAC offices, or by contacting the Croydon office (see page 94).

Opening times

Museums, churches and archaeological sites usually close over the lunch break from 12 noon to 3 pm. Many museums close on Mondays; entrance is sometimes free on Sundays.

Banks normally open on weekdays from 8.30 am to 1.30 pm and for an hour in the early afternoon, though this varies from bank to bank. They are closed on Saturdays and Sundays. There are bureaux de change in the larger tourist centres which open at weekends, but they generally offer a poor rate of exchange.

Shops are normally open Monday to Friday from 9 am to 1 pm and from 4.30 to 7 pm. In the popular holiday resorts many shops stay open longer in the evening and are open on Sundays and public holidays.

Petrol stations are usually closed between noon and 3 pm and from 7 pm.

Post and telephone

Stamps (*francobolli*) are bought at post offices and from tobacconists displaying a large T outside. Only standard envelopes should be used for letters. Post offices normally open on weekdays from 8.30 am to 5 pm and on Saturdays till 1 pm.

Public telephones are found in bars and shops displaying the yellow and black *Telefono pubblico* sign. Bars, newsagents, etc. also sell the tokens (*gettoni*) used for making a call (they cost 200 lire). The newer telephones — now fairly common — take 200 and 400 lire coins as well. A considerable number of coins and gettoni are needed for an international call. Calls made from hotels are expensive as there will be a surcharge to pay.

To telephone abroad dial 00 44 for Britain (01139 for the US/Canada), the area code minus the initial 0, then the subscriber number.

Public holidays

New Year: January 1st
Epiphany: January 6th
Easter Monday
Liberation Day: April 25th
Labour Day: May 1st
Feast of the Assumption (*Ferragosto*):
    August 15th

All Saints: November 1st
Immaculate Conception: December 8th
Christmas: December 25th and 26th

Time

Italy keeps Central European Time (GMT
+ 1 hour). Clocks are advanced a further
hour in summer, an hour ahead of British
Summer Time.

Tipping

Hotels and restaurants generally add a
fixed service charge to the bill (between
10 and 15%). A tip is expected on top of
that, however, and failure to give one will
be taken as an expression of dissatis-
faction.

If you stay for any length of time in a
hotel it will pay to give staff a 'mid-way'
tip. 15,000 lire each for the waiter and
chambermaid is about right for a fort-
night's stay in a medium-range hotel. For
all other services (e.g. hairdressers and
taxis) tips of 10 to 15% are expected.
N.B. The ordinary 'servizio' politely given
will get you much further than excessive
flamboyance with lire notes.

Touring by car

Distances on the main roads between
places in Tuscany and Umbria are relatively short. In the tours suggested below,
easy driving leaves plenty of time and
energy for brief visits to the towns en route.

Italy's main north-south motorway, the
Autostrada del Sole, crosses the whole of
Tuscany, passing Florence and Arezzo on
the way to Orvieto, where it brushes the
south-west corner of Umbria. (*Autostrade*
incidentally are toll roads; tolls may be
paid in cash or, in many cases, with a
Viacard, obtainable from motorway toll-
booths, tourist offices, tobacconists and
some banks.)

From Florence the Firenze–Mare
motorway joins up near Pisa with the SS 1
(the old Via Aurelia running along the
Tuscan coast). Just west of Florence at

Certosa the Autostrada del Sole is met by
the fast Siena road, which again joins up
with the Via Aurelia, this time at Grosseto.
South of Florence a fast road branches off
the Autostrada del Sole to rejoin it further
south near Terni (via Perugia and Spoleto).

Here now are one or two suggestions
for varying these routes in a more
leisurely holiday spirit, giving the unspoilt
countryside away from the major roads a
chance to work its spell.

**Pisa — Volterra — S. Gimignano —
Siena:** Leave Pisa driving east on the SS
67 to Pontedera, branching off there onto
the SS 439 for Volterra. After looking
round Volterra take the small, twisting
but short stretch of road (c. 20 km) to
S. Gimignano. From S. Gimignano either
turn north for a short detour to nearby
Certaldo (then south to Poggibonsi), or
drive direct to Poggibonsi to join the
superstrada to Siena.

Florence — Arezzo — Perugia: Follow
the Autostrada del Sole to the Arezzo exit.
After visiting Arezzo take the SS 71 driving
past Castiglion Fiorentino to Cortona
(c. 30 km). Having seen Cortona rejoin the
SS 71 and continue to Terontola on Lake
Trasimene, where the road joins the SS
75 bis to Perugia.

Perugia — Assisi — Gubbio: From
Perugia it is only 26 km on the SS 147 to
Assisi. Having explored Assisi drive back
towards Perugia, turning north onto the
SS 3 bis (Via Flaminia). Shortly before
Umbertide (which should be visited) the
SS 219 turns off for Gubbio. The SS 298
offers a more difficult but very pleasant
alternative route to Gubbio via Mengara,
the turn-off being just north of Perugia.

**Perugia — Assisi — Spello —
Foligno — Spoleto:** Assisi is soon
reached from Perugia along the wide SS
147. After looking round Assisi take the SS
147b south, joining up with the SS 75 for
the short drive to Spello and on to Foligno.

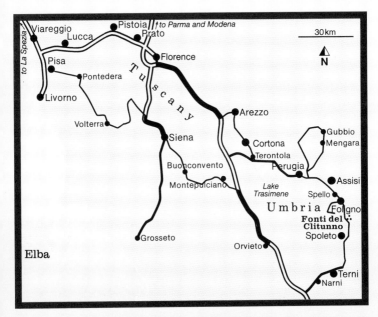

Here a detour should be made (14 km) to Bevagna and — with a few bends on the way — Montefalco. Then go back northwards to rejoin the SS 3 (Via Flaminia) before driving south via Trevi (situated on a hillside above the road) to pause at the picturesque spot where the Fonti del Clitunno (underground springs) form an attractive lake. It is then only another 10 km to Spoleto, beyond which the Via Flaminia continues to Terni and Narni, rejoining the Autostrada del Sole at Orte.

Siena — Pienza — Montepulciano — Chianciano — Orvieto: Leave Siena on the wide but winding SS 2 (Via Cassia), driving first to Buonconvento (c. 30 km) and then on to S. Quirico d'Orcia (44 km). Branch off left here onto the very twisting SS 146 to the little town of Pienza (10 km). Afterwards continue on the SS 146 to Montepulciano and Chianciano Terme from where it is an easy drive to Chiusi on the Autostrada del Sole, which cuts through the valley to Orvieto.

Car hire

The major international companies have offices in the larger towns and cities in the region. Many tour operators offer 'Fly-Drive' holidays, in which car hire is included.

Traffic regulations

Vehicles travel on the right. Seat belts must be worn in front seats, and children aged 4 to 10 must occupy seats with seat belts or other restraining device. Vehicles must be fitted with an outside mirror on the left side, and a nationality plate on the back. It is also obligatory to carry a warning triangle and a spare set of bulbs for lights and indicators.

In towns, traffic coming from the right has priority. In the country, main-road traffic has priority unless signs show otherwise. Drivers must signal their intention to change lanes or overtake. In towns the horn should only be used in an emergency. **Do not** drink and drive.

Speed limits: built-up areas 31 mph (50 kph), outside built-up areas 56 mph (90 kph). Motorway speed limits vary according to engine size. Cars up to 1090 cc/motorcycles up to 349 cc: 68 mph/110 kph; cars over 1100 cc/ motorcycles over 349 cc: 81 mph/ 130 kph. Cars towing caravans are limited to 50 mph/80 kph outside built-up areas and 62 mph/100 kph on motorways.

Fuel for private motor vehicles must only be carried in the tank fitted to the vehicle. It is forbidden to carry spare fuel, and to fill fuel cans at a petrol station. Petrol tokens offering a discount on the normal price of petrol can be purchased from the RAC and at frontier crossing-points.

Important addresses
Diplomatic and consular offices
British Embassy
80a Via XX Settembre
00187 Roma;
tel. 06/4 755 441, 4 755 551

British Consulate
Palazzo Castelbarco
2 Lungarno Corsini
50123 Firenze;
tel. 055/212 594

United States Embassy
119a Via Vittorio Veneto
00187 Roma;
tel. 06/4 674

United States Consulate
38 Lungarno Amerigo Vespucci
50100 Firenze;
tel. 055/298 276

Australian Embassy
215 Via Alessandria
00198 Roma;
tel. 06/832 721

Canadian Embassy
27 Via G. B. de Rossi
00161 Roma;
tel. 06/841 341

Irish Embassy
3 Largo del Nazareno
00187 Roma;
tel. 06/6 782 541

New Zealand Embassy
28 Via Zara
00198 Roma;
tel. 06/4 402 928

Tourist information offices
In Italy
Azienda Autonoma di Turismo
(Firenze) 15 Via Tornabuoni
tel. 055/216 544

Ente Provinciale per il Turismo
(Firenze) 16 Via Manzoni
tel. 055/2 478 141

In UK
Italian State Tourist Office (ENIT)
1 Princes Street
London W1R 8AY;
tel. 071 408 1254

In United States
Italian State Tourist Office
630 Fifth Avenue, Suite 1565
New York, NY10111;
tel. 212 245 4822–24

Information, brochures and accommodation lists can be obtained from the Italian State Tourist Office.

There are local tourist offices (Azienda Autonoma di Turismo) in the larger towns and resorts. Look for the **i** (= *informazione*) sign displayed outside.

RAC
RAC Motoring Services Ltd
RAC House
PO Box 100
South Croydon CR2 6XW;
tel. 081 686 2525

Useful words and phrases

Although English is often understood in the parts of Italy frequented by tourists, the visitor will undoubtedly find a few words and phrases of Italian very useful.

please	per favore
thank you (very much)	(molte) grazie
yes/no	si/no
excuse me	scusi (I beg your pardon), con permesso (when passing in front of someone)
do you speak English?	parla inglese?
I do not understand	non capisco
good morning	buon giorno
good evening	buona sera
goodbye	arrivederci
how much?	quanto?
I should like	vorrei avere
a room with a private bath	una camera con bagno
the bill, please (in restaurant)	cameriere, il conto!
everything included	tutto compreso
when?	quando?
open	aperto
shut	chiuso
where is .... street?	dov'è la via ...?
the road to?	la strada per ...?
how far is it to...	quanto è distante ...?
to the left/right	a sinistra/a destra
straight on	sempre diritto
post office	ufficio postale
railway station	stazione
town hall	municipio
exchange office	ufficio di cambio
police station	posto di polizia
public telephone	telefono pubblico
tourist information office	ufficio turistico
doctor	medico
chemist's	farmacia
toilet	gabinetto
ladies	signore
gentlemen	signori
engaged	occupato
free	libero
entrance	entrata
exit	uscita
today/tomorrow	oggi/domani
Sunday/Monday	domenica/lunedì
Tuesday/Wednesday	martedì/mercoledì
Thursday/Friday	giovedì/venerdì
Saturday/holiday	sabato/giorno festivo

0	zero
1	uno, una, un, un'
2	due
3	tre
4	quattro
5	cinque
6	sei
7	sette
8	otto
9	nove
10	dieci
11	undici
12	dodici
20	venti
50	cinquanta
100	cento

Torre del Mangia, Siena

Index